THE
OBELISK
AND
FREEMASONRY

ACCORDING TO THE DISCOVERIES

OF

BELZONI AND COMMANDER GORRINGE.

ALSO

EGYPTIAN SYMBOLS COMPARED WITH THOSE DISCOVERED
IN AMERICAN MOUNDS.

BY

JOHN A. WEISSE, M.D.,

Author of " Origin, Progress and Destiny of the English Language and Literature."

WITH

COLORED AND PLAIN ILLUSTRATIONS, THE HIEROGLYPHS OF THE
AMERICAN AND ENGLISH OBELISKS, AND TRANSLATIONS
INTO ENGLISH BY DR. S. BIRCH.

ISBN: 978-1-63923-931-3

All Rights reserved. No part of this book maybe reproduced without written permission from the publishers, except by a reviewer who may quote brief passages in a review to be printed in a newspaper or magazine.

Printed: March 2023

Published and Distributed By:
Lushena Books
607 Country Club Drive, Unit E
Bensenville, IL 60106
www.lushenabks.com

ISBN: 978-1-63923-931-3

The Obelisk as it stood at Alexandria.
(*From "Ebers' Egypt."*)

To the
MASONIC FRATERNITY
ALL OVER THE GLOBE
This Epitome is Dedicated,

BY THE AUTHOR.

PREFACE.

As our Secretary of State, Mr. Evarts, considered Commander Gorringe's discoveries on the *Obelisk* of sufficient importance to open a correspondence between the State Department and our Consul-General, Mr. Farman, we feel encouraged that the manuscripts, drawings, etc., presented to us by Mrs. Belzoni, at Brussels, 1850, will corroborate Commander Gorringe's opinions, and prove that an institution, similar to *Freemasonry*, existed in Egypt before *pyramids* and *obelisks;* because the Masonic tools, *perpendicular, square, compass, plummet,* etc., were required to construct Egypt's architectural wonders, and must therefore have antedated those wonders. Moreover, these implements must have been used in building Babel, Nineveh, and Babel's Tower in the valley of the Euphrates. The article on Belzoni's manuscripts and drawings, published by the New York Herald, February 16, 1880, attracted much attention and elicited letters from the far West; so did Consul Farman's erudite and graphic paper, now in the State Department, among the national archives; it was published by the New York World, April 21, 1880.

In this epitome we shall quote Belzoni's manuscripts on Egyptian Freemasonry, illustrated by colored drawings, as found on the walls of the rock-excavated Masonic Temple, constructed by Pharaoh Seti I. (*Osymandias*) and his son Rameses II. (*Sesostris*). Any one who will take the trouble to read this epitome and consider its illustrations, will realize that secret societies like Freemasonry existed in remote antiquity, and were the prerogative of kings, hierophants, and magnates.

We must not omit to express our heartfelt thanks to those whose works, lectures, and conversations enabled us to write this epitome: Champollion, Dr. Young, Spohn, Bunsen, Gliddon, Lepsius, De Rougé, Wilkinson, Poole, Ebers, Birch, Chabas, Brugsch, Mariette, Maspéro, Macoy, Rawson, Amelia Edwards, London Athenæum, Spohn's pupil, Seyffarth, who has been among us in New York for many years, and Mackenzie, whose *Royal Masonic Cyclopædia*,* recently published by J. W. Bouton, of New York, furnished us most valuable information.

Freemasonry, as connected with Belzoni's grand Masonic Temple found in 1818, and with Commander Gorringe's discovery of Masonic emblems and symbols on the obelisk now (June 16, 1880) on its way to New York, will be our chief aim.

We shall also mention the 5 obelisks yet standing in Egypt, and relate the adventures of the 11 now in Rome; 3 elsewhere in Italy; 2 in Constantinople; 2 in France; 6 in England; 1 on its way to America; and of the one in Germany, which, though the smallest of the 30, is the oldest, being coeval with the Fifth Manethonian Dynasty, which, according to Brugsch, † reigned " 3700 *to* 3300 B.C."

As in Egypt, Pharaohs, princes, hierophants, and magnates were masons, engineers, and architects, Freemasons of our day may look with pride toward the cradle of civilization, of which the coming obelisk will be a worthy representative in the New World.

JOHN A. WEISSE, M.D.

30 WEST FIFTEENTH STREET,
    NEW YORK, June 16, 1880.

---

* This octavo of 782 pages is really a Thesaurus, not only for Freemasons, but for scholars generally.

† "History of Egypt," p. 68.

INTRODUCTION.

THE OBELISK.

This word is derived from Greek οβελισκος (*spit* or *broach*), whence also Latin *obeliscus*, French *obélisque*, German *obelisk*, etc. Under the earliest Pharaohs the Egyptian or (Coptic) word for obelisk was *Tekhen ;* but after the Twenty-second Dynasty it was called *Men*, which meant *stability*. Another ancient Egyptian term for obelisk was *Djeri Anschaï, which means "written column,"* an appellation quite significant and sacred in the Coptic language.

An obelisk is a four-sided pillar tapering from the base, and terminating, not in a flat surface, but in a *pyramidion*, which is the diminutive for pyramid. It is usually of one piece, styled *monolith* (one stone). Originally these monoliths were used as funeral monuments, and were either of sandstone, limestone, or granite. Later they were of rose-colored granite, composed of *quartz, feldspar*, and *hornblende.* This granite was named *syenite*, from *Syene*, a city in Upper Egypt, where those beautiful monoliths were quarried. They were placed on pedestals before gateways of the principal temples in Egypt, one on each side of the door ; thus, an obelisk consists of a *pedestal, shaft*, and *pyramidion*, which terminates in an *apex*.

The artistic rules for the construction of an Egyptian obelisk are : the length of one of the four base-lines measures one-tenth of the length of the shaft ; so the pyramidion is one-tenth of the shaft, and forms a graceful top for the whole structure, all in keeping with the tapering shaft and pedestal, which slightly projects beyond the base of the shaft. [The Egyptians had observed, that the play of the sunbeams on a polished surface made it appear *concave*, although it was perfectly level and smooth, and gave to the face a *convexity* exactly proportionate to that optical illusion. The convexity of the obelisk of Luxor, in Paris, which appears absolutely level, is 16 lines in the centre. This simple detail clearly shows a minute observation and a very advanced art. Thus their slightly *convex* sides increase their apparent height. The pyramidion, or apex, was made more pointed in some obelisks than in others. /

Most Egyptian obelisks bear hieroglyphic inscriptions: the four faces or sides are engraved with care, despite the hardness of the *syenite*, which must have presented immense difficulties, especially when we consider, that they had no tools and facilities as we have. Hieroglyphs are usually engraved on four sides from the top downward. There are three perpendicular rows on each side, the middle one of which is read first; then the one on the right; and next the one on the left. Thus, the translators of obelistic hieroglyphs pass from side to side and then adjust the whole. On the obelisk of Luxor, in Paris, the medial inscription of three of the sides is dedicated to Rameses II.; whereas the two lateral of these three sides and the fourth entire side are about Rameses III., who caused the work to be completed. The work of the engraver also differs: the inscriptions of the middle column are deeply cut; whereas those of the lateral columns have less depth by one-half. This arrangement, thus contrived, is of a harmonious symmetry.*

The gracefully proportioned pillar, styled obelisk, was coëval with budding Egyptian art; for we find it from the

---

* We give these details to enable readers to understand the modus operandi of Egyptologists, who translate the inscriptions on obelisks. Moreover, when they glance at an obelisk, they will know how the Egyptians read ages ago.

Fourth and Fifth Manethonian Dynasties (3700 to 3300 B.C.*) to the Roman sway under Domitian, A.D. 132. Obelisks were not only used as monuments to the gods and the dead, but for recording the deeds and reigns of Pharaohs; but, besides these devotional purposes, they had a practical object, and served as *gnomons* or *hands*, whose shadow was made to indicate the hours of the day,† as will appear in the course of this epitome.

In the first century of our era Pliny wrote: "Monarchs entered into a kind of rivalry in forming elongated blocks of this stone, known as *obelisks*, and consecrated them to the divinity of the *sun*. The blocks had this form given to them in resemblance to the rays of that luminary, which are so called in the Egyptian language." The Roman archeologist little dreamed that, nineteen centuries after he penned these lines, modern savants would decipher from hieroglyphs *Sati*, which is the name of an Egyptian goddess, and means *sun-beam*.

Thus we realize, that the obelisk was connected with sun-worship. The Greek *stelæ* and Roman columns were probably derived therefrom. Solomon's two pillars, *Jachin* and *Boaz*, were but an imitation of two obelisks at the entrance of Egyptian temples; so are the two towers on Gothic cathedrals and two steeples on churches. Perhaps Ovid's "Philemon and *Baucis*" were borrowed from Solomon's Temple, *Baucis* being only a linguistic namesake of *Boaz?*

No wonder obelisks, cherished during four thousand years, now adorn *Greenwood*, *Auburn*, *All Souls*, *Père la Chaise*, where their ethereal *pyramidions* are legion. New Yorkers

---

* Brugsch's "History of Egypt," p. 68.
† Voltaire, speaking of ancient *horology*, observes: "*But our meridians are more just than those of antiquity.*" Had the author of "*Charles XII.*" and "*Zaïre*" thought before he penned this sentence, he would have realized, that he was telling the world nothing new or striking; for mankind had about two thousand years to progress in geography, meridians, and astronomy.

showed their predilection for obelisks in the "*Worth Monument,*" near the crossing of Fifth Avenue and Broadway. As a Christian emblem, the obelisk typifies resurrection. *Freemasons* use it in symbolic degrees.

Ages ago Solon, Thales, Pythagoras, Plato, Herodotus,* Germanicus,† etc., conversed with the Egyptian hierophants and priests concerning Egypt's history and architectural wonders. But their account remained meagre and vague, till lately Champollion, Young, Spohn, Seyffarth, Belzoni, de Rougé, Bunsen, Gliddon, Rawlinson, Lepsius, Mariette, Brugsch, Ebers, Chabas, Maspéro, Birch, and Commander Gorringe interrogated hieroglyphic, hieratic, and demotic characters, signs, emblems, and symbols, which directly and indirectly answered more satisfactorily than the hierophants of old, together with Moses, Herodotus, Manetho, Pliny, Strabo, and Tacitus; yea, daily and yearly those silent signs and symbols on pyramids, *obelisks*, temples, and tombs reveal the arcana and history of primitive heroes, families, tribes, nations, dynasties, and empires. Even Masonic attitudes, postures, initiations, and regalia are being divined and ascertained, since figures on the walls of unearthed palaces, temples, and tombs tell the story of their long-departed inmates, as may be seen in the vast subterranean temple discovered by Belzoni. In this epitome we shall endeavor to show what Egypt has been, is, and will be to those, who sincerely search for mankind's primitive history. Ancient statesmen, sages, historians, and artists visited Egypt to study her social status and admire her architectural wonders. Mediæval alchemists and savans looked to Egypt as the source of their theories. Egyptologists have been trying for the last fifty years to unravel Egypt's hieroglyphs; and now the earliest society for mutual protection and charity—Freemasonry—points to Egyptian obelisks and splendid rock-excavated temples as repositories of its secrets.

---

* Herodotus, B. II., 111.
† Tacitus' Annals, B. II., 59.

THE
OBELISK AND FREEMASONRY.

CHAPTER I.

"The Egyptians stand forth pre-eminently as the monumental people of the world."
—BUNSEN.

BEFORE we approach Freemasonry in this epitome, we shall give all that concerns the *obelisk*, destined to adorn the American metropolis. We have scanned journals and periodicals, and gleaned from them what appeared most appropriate and interesting to readers. First and foremost comes the masterly report, illustrations, and measurements * by Grand Master S. A. Zola, and the accompanying conversations, published in the New York Herald, April 23, 1880.

Mr. Zola is Sovereign Grand Commander of the Supreme Council of the Ancient and Accepted Scottish Rite, Past Grand Master of the National Grand Lodge of Egypt, and Chief of the Symbolic Masonry of Egypt.

This report is an answer to hundreds of letters Mr. Zola received from masons in all parts of the globe.

---

* To enable readers to realize the true dimensions of the obelisk, its pedestal and objects connected therewith, we reduced Grand Master Zola's French into English measures, which was rather disagreeable labor, especially when we consider, that *uniform measures and weights* would remove one of the chief barriers to easy and cheap national intercourse, which, as we show in our "Origin, *Progress, and Destiny of the English Language and Literature,*" pp. 680–686, would be an immense stride towards free trade and a *universal language*.

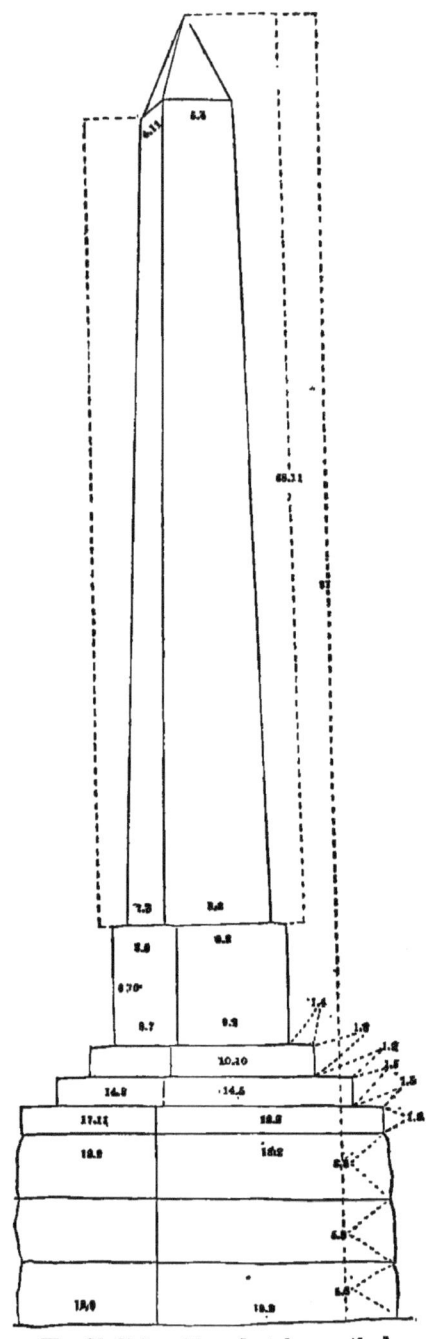

The Obelisk, with pedestal unearthed.

THE REPORT.

Report by Ill∴ Bro∴ S. A. Zola, 33 S∴ G∴ Com∴ upon the discoveries made by Bro∴ Lieutenant-Commander Gorringe and himself at the base of Cleopatra's Needle:

Having learned that some stones bearing Masonic symbols had been brought to light by Lieutenant-Commander Gorringe, I presented myself to him and accepted the offer courteously made to assist at the work, inspect the stones discovered, and express my opinion as to their Masonic signification. Bro. Gorringe, being occupied with the more difficult part of the task entrusted to him, requested me to make further researches.

The obelisk known as Cleopatra's Needle was erected on a pedestal, almost a cube, from the surface of which it was raised 9½ in., and was supported by four square axes five centimetres thick. Two of these axes ran through crabs, while the other two had been sawn off and removed in days gone by.

The height of the perpendicular of the obelisk from its apex to its base is 68 ft. 11 in., and the perpendicular of the sides is 64 feet. In volume it is 2,678 cubic feet, and in weight about 186 tons.

One of the sides is 5 ft. 4 in. wide at the top and 8 ft. 3 in. at the base; its parallel 5 ft. 3 in. and 8 ft. 3 in. at the base. Another side is 5 ft. wide at the top and 7 ft. 8 in. at the base; its parallel 4 ft. 10 in. and 7 ft. 8 in. at the base.

The pedestal is 6 ft. 10 in. high; one of the sides measures 9 ft. 2 in. at the top and base, its parallel 8 ft. 9 in. at the top and 8 ft. 7 in. at base; a third size is 9 ft. at top and 9 ft. 2 in. at base, its parallel has 8 ft. 9 in. at top and 8 ft. 7 in. at base. This pedestal rested on three steps, the upper two of which are formed of four blocks, while the first step is formed of eighteen stones.. These steps are of white, hard stone.

The length of the step under the pedestal varies from 10

ft. 10 in. to 12 ft. 3 in., its depth from 1 ft. 2 in. to 1 ft. 8 in., its height from 1 ft. 3 in. to 1 ft. 3¼ in.

The length of the step immediately under the above varies from 14 ft. 3 in. to 14 ft. 8 in., its depth from 1 ft. 2 in. to 1 ft. 6 in., its height from 1 ft. 5 in. to 1 ft. 6 in.

The length of the third step varies from 17 ft. 11 in. to

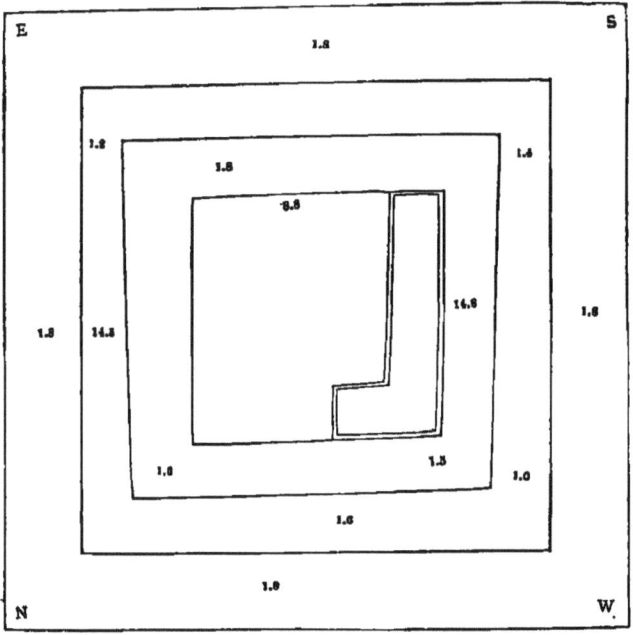

18 ft. 2 in., its depth from 1 ft. 5 in. to 1 ft. 9 in., its height 1 ft. 8 in.

The foundations consist of three rows of six stones each per side, thus forming a rectangular parallelogram. The stones are rough and irregular.

These foundations have a depth of about 5 ft. 3 in., while the sides have a length of about 18 ft. 2 in. at the top and about 19 ft. 2 in. at the bottom.

The perpendicular of the edifice from the apex to the base of the foundation is 96 ft. It should be remarked that the present level of Alexandria is about 20 feet higher than that of the ancient city. The present level of the sea is about 5 ft. 10 in. higher than the ancient level of the sea.

A and A'.—*The " Gorringe" Stone No.* 1 was found last January inside the foundation of the obelisk, and on a line running from west to east. In form it is a rectangular parallelogram, having two sides partially worked and partially finished and polished. The lower surface finished and polished, the upper surface and remaining two sides in a rough state. On the two partially finished sides and by the line

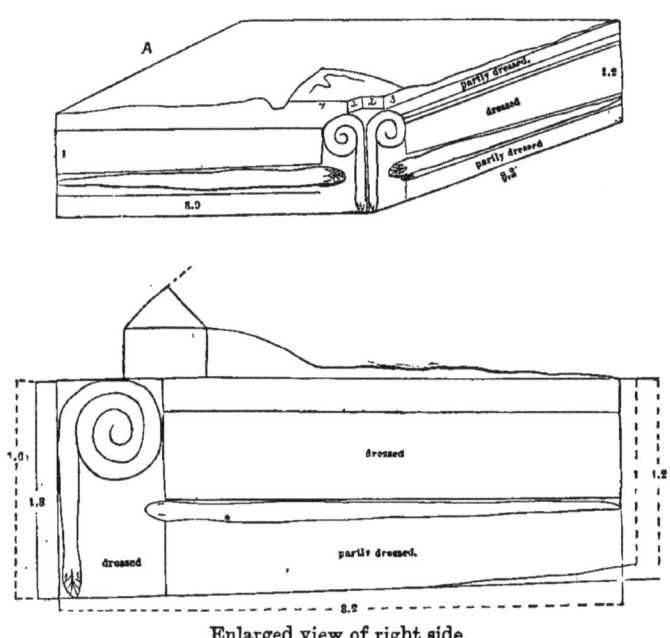

Enlarged view of right side.

forming the angle, are two serpents about two-thirds coiled, heads downward, meeting toward and reaching to the lower line. Toward the middle of the same sides are two other serpents with the heads turned toward the same angle.

Dimensions.—The stone is 3 ft. 9 in. long, 3 ft. 2 in. wide, and three of the corners are each 1 ft. 3 in. high and the fourth 1 ft. 2 in. Above the coils of the serpents and at the point where the two upper lines should meet, is cut in a right angle with the following measures:—Right side, 2 in. high, 2 in. deep, 7 in. long, the remaining portion being rough; left side, 3½ in. high, 3 in. deep, 1 ft. 5 in. long.

Signification.—I consider this a piece of architecture, offering at a glance the labors of the three symbolic degrees —the apprentice's being represented by the rough parts, the craftsman's by the worked portions, and the master's by the finished and ornamented parts of the stone. It should be remarked that, in the stone itself, the coiled serpents have not the head and the horizontal ones are completely lacking; but their traces are so clear, that I could easily restore them, and was thus enabled carefully to measure them. The extremity, moreover, of one of the heads is still visible. These ornaments have a relief of about four lines.

B.—"*Gorringe*" *Stone No.* 2 was found at about the same time, inside a pit, corresponding to the axis of the obelisk.

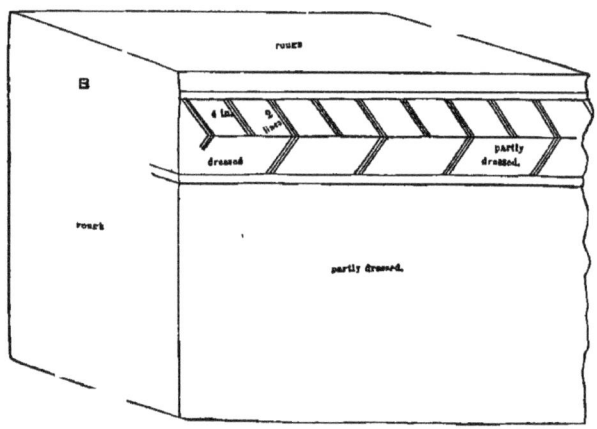

It stood near stone A, but toward the west. In shape it is an irregular parallelogram. Five of the faces are rough, while the surface of the sixth is partly roughened down, in part dressed and the rest finished. The upper portion of this surface is 3 lines thicker than the rest. The first half of the said upper portion has, at different distances, ten double oblique cuttings, almost parallel. (See drawing.) The length of the cuttings is 4 in., their width 2 lines.

Signification.—This may be a tracing-stone representing the labors of the three degrees, and also, probably, a sketch of the linear measure of those days.

C.—"*Gorringe*" *Stone No. 3.*—This was found near A, but placed more toward the west. In form it is a rectangular parallelogram and all its faces are roughened down. Toward the angle of one of its faces and pointing to it was found a thoroughly oxidized metallic trowel, rather larger than those at present in use. I did not see it entire, because three or four days after it was discovered the stone was broken and three-fourths of the upper part of the trowel

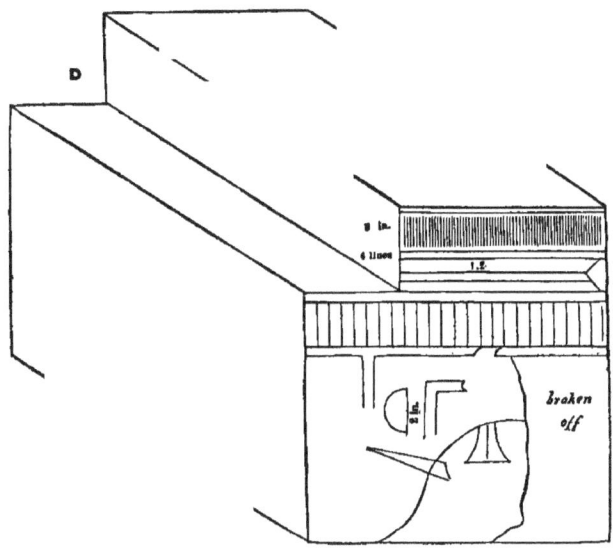

were taken away, leaving only the portion near the handle. A second theft was subsequently committed, and there now remains only a portion of the handle of the trowel. The stone is 3 ft. 11 in. long, 2 ft. 2 in. thick, and 1 ft. 3 in. high.

Signification.—Considering the roughened state of the stone and its proximity to stone A, and more especially toward the imperfect faces of the latter, I regard this stone as representing the apprentice and fellow-craft, while the presence of the trowel is emblematical of the master.

D.—Stone discovered by Brother Zola near B, but placed toward the east in the angle of the pit, forming a square. This stone presents the appearance of a parallelogram superposed on another, thus forming a step. Four faces are rough, while the two forming the step are roughened down and the base of the step is rough. Of the remaining face—the side of the step—the upper portion about two-thirds of the total height is rough, the remaining portion being perfectly finished and polished. The latter portion is divided horizontally into three equal parts, which, cut at obtuse angles at the end opposite the step, represent the model of an hexagonal column. Immediately under this representation and parallel thereto is a line in relief on the whole length of the surface. The distances between the lines forming the model are 4 lines and $4\frac{1}{2}$ lines; their length varies from $8\frac{1}{2}$ to 9 in. The thickness of the lower line is 1 line and the length 1 ft. 2 in. Under this line are placed in a row, at right angles with this face, twenty quadrilateroids having a relief of about 1 line. They are $1\frac{1}{2}$ in. high and 5 lines and 6 lines at the top, and 5 lines and 6 lines at the bottom, every alternate two being equal.

These quadrilateroids are confined at the base by another parallel line, which, with a perpendicular line at right angles, placed under the third quadrilateroid, forms a square the horizontal line of which reaches the middle of the twelfth quadrilateral, and measures 7 in., while the perpendicular has a length of $3\frac{1}{2}$ in. The width of the angle at the perpendicular side of this square is $5\frac{1}{2}$ lines, while at the end of the same side it is 6 lines. The width ($5\frac{1}{2}$ lines) above noted corresponds to the uneven numbers of the quadrilateroids, while toward the angle formed by the horizontal line, and precisely under the quadrilateroid formed by even numbers, the width is 5 lines. At a distance 1 in. and 2 lines from the horizontal line of the square and at $1\frac{1}{2}$ lines from the perpendicular side, is a perfect semicircle, having a relief of 1 line and a diameter of 2 inches. At 10 lines from the diameter of the semicircle, and at 11 lines from the horizontal side of the square, is seen another square having a horizontal line of 10 in. and a perpendicular line of 2½ in. The width of the angle is 2½ lines, at the end of the horizontal line 3 lines, and at the end of the perpendicular 3 in. At a short distance from the latter square is seen a level, formed by two segments, having a radius of 1 in., a horizontal line 2½ in. in length and perpendicular 1¾ in.

This level is 1 line in relief. In the centre of the horizontal line is a semicircle, having a radius of about 1 line. The length of this line is, therefore, equal to the long side of the small square. Under the level is visible another emblem or part of one formed by a horizontal line and a curve, which form an acute angle in the shape of a wedge with a relief of 1 line. The horizontal line is 4 in. in length and the curve is about the same.

Signification.—To my mind this stone, because of the rough, partly wrought and entirely finished parts, is also, whether taken by itself or in conjunction with the emblems cut upon it, emblematical of the symbolic degrees. The equilateroids, moreover, represent the proportions of the stones thus far discovered, and also of the whole edifice. This, therefore, was the general model by which the master tested the skill and proficiency of the craftsmen in the royal art.

I should not omit here to mention, that a perfect model was found in black granite of the hexagonal column above described.

Note.—Having sketched this stone, I returned on the 7th of March to compare my sketch. While thus engaged I noticed a stranger coming toward me, and I concealed the stone with a view to make an agreeable surprise to Brother Gorringe. On the following day I showed him my sketch, but to our great astonishment, a portion of the stone near the level had been broken off.

E.—This is a block of Syenite granite similar to that of which the obelisk is made. It was found by Brother Gorringe in the interior of the foundations. In shape it is a cube, and its faces are carefully dressed and finished. It is 3 ft. 6 in. long, 3 ft. 5½ in. high, and 2 ft. 8½ thick.

Signification.—Judging from the shape and dimensions of the stone, as well as from its situation (between the east angle of the chamber and the east angle of the pit), this stone, to my mind, represents the perfect ashlar.

F.—This block is also of syenite granite. It is in shape a rectangular parallelogram. It was found by Bro. Gorringe in the interior of the chamber, between east and west. Four of its faces are rough, one finished, and the last roughened down. This stone is 5 ft. 3 in. in length, 3 ft. 5½ in. in height, and 1 ft. 4 in. in thickness.

Signification.—This, I think, is meant to represent the rough ashlar, as well as the work of the three degrees.

G.—In the interior of the foundations and under the first step Bro. Gorringe found a square, one side of which (the shorter) ran from west to north and the other from west to south. This square is also of syenite granite, cut in a block 2 ft. 1 in. thick, 8 ft. 9 in. long, and 4 ft. 3 in. wide. The cutting is 8½ in. deep and the inner sides of the square are ornamented with three parallel lines, forming three steps. These lines are 2 in. thick. The larger side is 1 ft. 6½ in. wide, reaching to 1 ft. 7½ in. at the angle, while the other is 1 ft. 5 in. at the angle and 1 ft. 5 in. at the end.

H.—A perfectly white stone found by Brother Gorringe in the centre of the eighteen stones, forming the first step. This stone—in shape a rectangular parallelogram—is calcareous, and, at first sight, of light brown color, but on breaking, it presents a milky white appearance. It was found near the cube, and has the following dimensions: length, 4 ft. 1 in..; width, 2 ft. ; thickness, 8 in.

This stone presents a curious phenomenon. It darkens perceptibly at the touch, and on exposure to the air. The natives know it by the appellation of the " milky stone," and ascribe to it the virtue of facilitating milk in cases of confinement. This stone is supposed to have been held· sacred by the ancient Egyptians, as a symbol of the sun and of other celestial bodies. I think that it is meant to represent the purity, that should distinguish the applicant for initiation.

I.—The interior of the foundations form a chamber, a quadrilateroid in shape. One of the sides is 16 ft. 8½ in. wide, the second 16 ft. 3 in., the third 16 ft. 7¼ in., and the last 16 ft. 11 in. In the perimeter, formed by these sides,

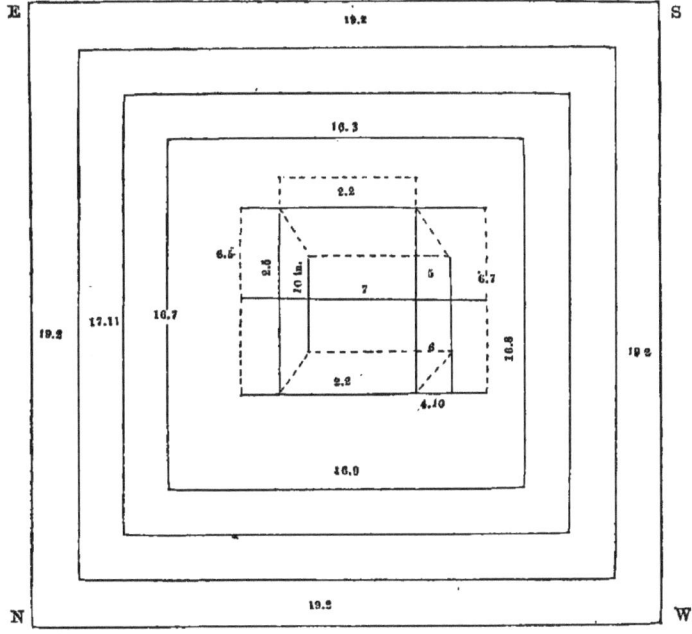

are three steps of calcareous stone and of granite. These steps, though not of the same dimensions, follow the lines of the outer steps.

In the centre of the chamber is a pit, made of rubble and calcareous stones, and covered with cement. At the eastern angle is built a wall in the form of a square. The longer side, 2 ft. 5½ in., running to the north, and the other, 2 ft. 2 in., extending to the south. The width of the longer side is 10 in. 3 lines, and the other 1 ft. 3. in. This pit is also a quadrilateroid, one of the sides measuring 4 ft. 10 in., its parallel 4 ft. 1 in. The third side, 6 ft. 6 in., and the fourth, 6 ft. 3 in.

As the exavations are not completed, I reserve to give further details or rectify any errors, when the work is finished.

Le Grand Commandeur Sup∴ Coun∴ d'Egypte.

S. A. ZOLA, 33∴

ALEXANDRIA, EGYPT, March 22, 1880.

NOTE.—It will be observed, that C (stone with trowel), E (perfect ashlar), F (rough ashlar), and H (pure white stone), are not represented in the sketches, because, being simple blocks without intricate cuttings, they are sufficiently described in the text of the report.

THE VIEWS OF MARIETTE PACHA.

On March 24th your correspondent called at the newly restored Museum of Egyptian Antiquities at Boulac, near Cairo, on the banks of the Nile. The object of my visit was to hear what Mariette Pacha, who at present lives at the Museum, might have to say about the now famous stones, found by Lieutenant-Commander Gorringe underneath the Cleopatra Needle. Mariette Pacha's claims to the highest rank as an Egyptologist need not be set forth here. Suffice it to say—and I think this will be pretty generally conceded—that the two living Egyptologists, who stand head and shoulders above all others, are Henri Brugsch-Bey and Mariette Pacha. Brugsch-Bey, besides being an Egyptologist, is also a Freemason, but is unfortunately in Berlin, so that there will be delay before his views can be laid before the readers of the *Herald*. Upon being duly announced I was conducted to a large, pleasant room, overlooking the Nile, and decorated entirely in accordance with ancient Egyptian art. This is Mariette Pacha's study. Seated at a table near the middle of the room, and earnestly contemplating various models of Egyptian antiquities, I found the

Pacha. Above the middle height and size, snow-white hair, mustache and beard; prominent nose, bright, intelligent eyes, Mariette Pacha—were it not for his florid complexion—would have the appearance of the typical antiquarian. He always wears the rosette of the Légion d'Honneur, and, when in Egypt, wears the tarboosh (Egyptian fez), which causes the eminent Egyptologist to resemble the finest and handsomest types of the Turkish pachas. Mariette Pacha is at present in very feeble health. His eyes have to be protected by smoked spectacles, and his voice is very much affected by bronchitis. I was accompanied during this visit by Dr. Fanton, who on that same day (March 24th) had arrived in Cairo by rail, leaving Prince Osman Pacha at Siout. Dr. Fanton claims to have made most important discoveries at Denderah and Abydos, in relation to Freemasonry and the Mysteries of Osiris, and is now busy in working up his notes and sketches.

After a short preliminary conversation I asked the Pacha: —"What do you think of those stones, found under Cleopatra's Needle?"

MARIETTE PACHA (laughing incredulously)—Come, come; are you not sure but that there is some joke about them? Let us talk of something serious.

CORRESPONDENT—Are you a Freemason?

MARIETTE PACHA—No.

CORRESPONDENT—Some of the Freemasons think these stones are of the highest importance.

MARIETTE PACHA—Yes; and Prince Osman Pacha, who is not a Freemason, takes also an active interest in them. But somehow even the obelisk itself, under which the stones were found, has never seemed to be a really serious obelisk. In the first place it fell over at Heliopolis, then it went off to Alexandria to serve as a sort of plaything for Cleopatra, and now it is going to wander off *pour se prostituer* in America, far away from its native land.

The Pacha here showed us a plate from the famous work "L'Expédition Française en Égypte." This plate represented the Cleopatra's needle, the pedestal and the three steps underneath. The Pacha asked, "Where were these stones found?"

CORRESPONDENT—Inside the foundations underneath the lowest step. (The foundations are not represented in the plate, because they were not known to exist.)

MARIETTE PACHA—I could not venture to express an opinion upon them from verbal or written descriptions.

I promised to show the Pacha drawings or photographs of the stones as soon as they should be made, and alluded to the possible "Pickwickian" solution of the problem hinted at in an interview of a Herald correspondent with MM. Ernest Renan and Maspéro.

"Remember," rejoined the Pacha, "that those gentlemen are both true critics in the highest and broadest sense of the term—as such they are probably unequalled; but they are philologues and I am an archéologue, and shall look forward with great interest to the accurate representations of the stones, upon which I can base an opinion."

The following conversation then ensued between Mariette Pacha and Dr. Fanton:

DR. FANTON—I have returned to-day, Pacha, from Sioni by rail. Prince Osman Pacha has enabled me to make what I am sure will turn out to be discoveries of the highest importance. At Denderah and Abydos I have found distinctive marks and signs in the architecture of temples, which to my mind show, that these temples were simply Masonic temples—which strengthens the theory, that Freemasonry and the Mysteries of Osiris are identical, or nearly so.

MARIETTE PACHA—*Rêves insensés, mon cher docteur*. The Mysteries of Osiris I do not believe ever had an existence; certainly not, if we use "mysteries" in the strict acceptation of the term.

DR. FANTON—I see, Pacha, you don't put much faith in Herodotus.

MARIETTE PACHA—By no means. Herodotus was a man, who came here and traveled about at a time, when Egypt was under the influence of foreign nations. Egyptian history was ignored. All national pride and feeling had ceased to exist. Herodotus was often led into wild errors by persons, from whom he obtained his information—just as *les voyageurs anglais* are led into all sorts of absurdities by believing stories, told by their dragomans. In this way Herodotus has led us into all this nonsense about the "mysteries" of Osiris. Herodotus is by no means trustworthy (*véridique*), and has caused much mischief.

DR. FANTON—Nevertheless, Pacha, I shall not despair of proving my theory. In all questions of Egyptology we must all bow our heads to Mariette Pacha; but is it not possible that, in following a long course of study from a purely archæological standpoint, one may easily fail to observe views from an essentially different standpoint? By examining monuments from a Masonic point of view, I still hope to place at your disposition views, which may prove of great value to you as an archæologist.

MARIETTE PACHA—I wish you all success, but I must say I have serious doubts as to your reaching the desired result.

On March 29th, in company with Signor Zola, I again paid my respects to Mariette Pacha. The Pacha was so ill, that he could scarcely speak above a whisper. Signor Zola showed the drawings, which he had himself made, and which have already been sent to the Herald. Mariette Pacha did not remember to have come across any similar stones in the course of his long experience, and said, if the Freemasons can explain their signification, that would certainly be a great deal. Mariette Pacha desired, that models be made, so as to enable him to study them with greater advantage—a task which he intends to occupy himself with, as soon as his health will permit.

We cannot help adding to the preceding document and conversations, gleanings from the highly interesting despatch of Consul-General Farman to our Secretary of State, Mr. Evarts, as published in the New York World, April 21,

1880. They but confirm Commander Gorringe's discoveries, Grand Master Zola's report, and Dr. Fanton's opinions.

> AGENCY AND CONSULTATE-GENERAL
> OF THE UNITED STATES IN EGYPT,
> CAIRO, January 20, 1880.

"SIR—Referring to my despatches Nos. 301 and 344 of the 22d of June and 13th of November, 1879, relating to the obelisk, known as Cleopatra's Needle, I have the honor to communicate to you the following additional description of the foundations, on which the pedestal rested, with a statement of the discoveries, that have been made in their removal.

I also enclose a full translation of the hieroglyphs of the obelisk as far as they can be read, and give you such additional historical facts as I have been able to obtain, after considerable research, concerning this interesting monument.

The whole structure was a magnificent work, and shows that the architect Pontius would have been entitled, even at this day, to a position in the first rank of those of his profession. In the removal of the foundations there has been made what is considered a very important historical discovery, relating to the order of Freemasons, and confirming its claim of ancient origin. The stones, constituting the emblems referred to, had been removed before I saw them, and I shall leave it for Lieutenant-Commander Gorringe to give in his report to the department full particulars with drawings.

I will only state briefly what I saw, and give the positions of the stones according to the information, received from the Commander. All of the stone of the foundations, except the four pieces, which I shall hereafter mention, were of a light-colored limestone, slightly crystalline and approaching marble in its characteristics, and in some of its parts capable of a fair polish. On removing the pedestal, there was found under its southeasterly, or, perhaps more correctly, easterly corner (the four sides of the obelisk did not face the four cardinal points of the compass), a piece of red or syenitic granite forty-two inches square, and having its sides all carefully dressed and its angles right angles. Immediately under this granite block, and on the same plane with the lower step, was found a piece of white stone much thinner than the other blocks, and different from anything else in the foundation. This was also a limestone, and contained many small fossils, but it was all of the purest white. Below this there was another granite block, the upper part of which was cut in the form of a mason's square. Its long section was 8 ft. 6 in. by 1 ft. 5½ in., and its short section 4 ft. 3 in. by 1 ft. 7¾ in., measuring the length in each case from the outer angle of the square. It is 21½ in. thick, and would seem to have been originally a parallelogram 8 ft. 6 in. long by 4 ft. 3 in. broad, and the form of a mason's square, given to its upper surface by cutting out and lowering to the depth of nine inches that part of the stone, included between the two inner lines of the square, and the continuations of the transverse lines of its two ends. The lower part of the stone still has its original form of a parallelogram. The space cut out of its upper part was filled with the ordinary limestone of the foundations, so that on its first discovery only the upper surface in the form of a mason's square could be seen. The thinner part of the stone has been broken, perhaps by the unequal pressure, that came upon it, but the part forming the square is still perfect. The long section of the square lay very near, and nearly parallel to the southerly or southeasterly side of the foundations, in such a position, that its easterly or northeasterly end was directly under the white stone and the granite cube I have mentioned. In the same tier with the square and touching its short section in the west or westerly angle of the foundations, there was another block of syenitic granite, the upper surface of which was very irregular. It was about 3 ft. by 5 ft., but its angles were all different, and consequently no two of its sides parallel. On the same plane with the white stone, and adhering to the upper surface of a limestone block adjoining it, there was found an ordinary sized mason's trowel. It was of iron, almost wholly oxidized, and of the shape of a longitudinal section of an egg or of the flattened bowl of a spoon. The handle was about three-eighths of an inch in relief. The left side of the point of the blade was gone. All the rest is sufficiently perfect to be distinctly seen and at once unmistakably recognized. That it was an ordinary mason's trowel, made of iron or steel, there can be no doubt. The mortar or cement and the stone are of a similar color and of about the same hardness, and it appears to me, that a slight depression was cut in the stone and the trowel imbedded in the mortar. All of these symbols—the trowel, the square, the two granite blocks, which may be termed the perfect and the rough ashlars, and the white stone—are said to be in their correct positions as Masonic emblems. The fine emblems and their position cannot be considered as the result of chance. Their full import and historical importance will, however, be best understood and appreciated by the members of the Order of Freemasons. That the discovery is of historic value, I have no doubt. There are also a few cuttings on the foundations, which are not hieroglyphics, and which are said to be Masonic emblems, and which will be particularly described by Commander Gorringe.

There has been another important archæological discovery resulting from the excavations at the base of Cleopatra's Needle. This discovery was made by Mr. Dixon and the archæologist, Neroutsos Bey, on the 20th of June, 1877. An excavation was then made, sufficient to discover one of the crabs I have mentioned, and on the outside of its left claw, the only remaining claw of either crab, was found the following Greek inscription:

L. H. KAISAPOS
BAPBAPOS ANETHHKE
APXITEKTONOYNTOS
PONTIOY

The first letter of this inscription, L, represents the word "year," being the old form of *lambda*, which letter in this and similar cases is the initial of the word, which signifies "year." The second letter, H, represents the number 8, and the whole inscription may be translated as follows:

"In the year eight (of the reign) of Cæsar, Barbaros erected (dedicated) (this monument), Pontius being the architect."

On the inner side of the same claw was the following inscription in Latin:

ANNO VIII
AVGVSTI CAESARIS
BARBARVS PRAEF
AEGYPTI POSVIT
Archi-TecTante PonTio

that is to say: "In the year eight (of the reign) of Augustus Cæsar, Barbarus, Prefect of Egypt, erected (this monument) by the architect Pontius (Pontius being the architect)."

The above statements of Consul Farman fully endorse the opinions and ideas of the Masons and scholars, who investigated the Masonic signs and emblems on the Thothmes Obelisk. Thus is ancient history being unearthed, deciphered from monuments, and translated from hieroglyphic and cuneiform tablets and symbols by busy archeologic bees in all parts of the globe. The inscription on the crab's claw is of great importance, fixing as it does, the time of the obelisk's erection at Alexandria, and giving the name of the architect, Pontius, who must have been a Mason. Centuries hence Mr. Farman's despatch will reflect credit on our consular system, and be an honor to our State Department.

We think a short statement of the striking features of this ancient monument would assist the reader's memory; hence we give it before we introduce Dr. Birch's interesting remarks on the obelisk and his translation of the hieroglyphs:

28 THE OBELISK AND FREEMASONRY.

Whole height as it stood at Alexandria, including pedestal.......................... 96 ft.
Without pedestal (only the shaft)........... 68 ft. 11 in.
Base lines of the shaft.................... 8 ft. 3 in.
Top   "   "   " .... 5 ft. 4 in.
Mass or volume, about .... 2,678 cubic ft.
Weight, about............................ 186 tons.

As this and the London obelisk are considered twins, their dimensions, volume, and weight must be about the same.

DR. SAMUEL BIRCH'S REMARKS AND TRANSLATION OF THE HIEROGLYPHS.*

At one period of his reign, probably toward the close, Thothmes III., the great monarch of the Eighteenth Egyptian Dynasty, whose power extended from the confines of India to the islands of the Mediterranean and to the limits of equatorial Africa, erected several obelisks, to evince the greatness of his power or the depth of his piety, at Thebes and Heliopolis. Heliopolis was one of the great cities of Egypt, and divided the honors of a capital with the older Memphis, the site of the court of the Fourth and subsequent dynasties, and Thebes, which, founded at the Eleventh Dynasty, rose to be the capital of the Eighteenth Dynasty and those immediately succeeding. Heliopolis is known in the Egyptian texts as the city *par excellence* of obelisks, and the sole survivor still erect, which dates from the Twelfth Dynasty, shows they adorned the shrine of the god Tum. With the series of obelisks of Thothmes III. it is not the question here to deal, as a long and exhaustive essay on those monuments would take up too much space. It is the question of the obelisks, of Alexandria, two of which—one erect, the other fallen—formerly remained on the site of the ancient

---
* Published in "The London Athenæum," March 13, 1880, pp. 351 and 352.

port. The fallen one was removed to England in 1877, and erected on the Embankment, and an account of it was given in the Athenæum of that year. As the obelisk formerly erect is on its way to America, some account of it will not be inappropriate, as well as a translation of the four sides of the obelisk, so far as they can be made out, which will contain some addition to that of M. Chabas, contained in the little work of Mr. W. R. Cooper on obelisks.

Since the revival of learning, the obelisks of Alexandria had attracted the notice of students and travelers. During the sixteenth century Pierre du Balon, Thévenot, Le Brun, Radzivil, Evesham, Sandys, and Pietro de la Valle mention these obelisks, as the Arab Edrizi had done in the middle of the twelfth century; in the seventeenth century Bremond and Monconys. At the commencement of the eighteenth century, Paul Lucas saw these obelisks; Le Maire, Dominique Jauna, the Baron de Tott, Van Egmont, Heyman, Pococke, and Savary had visited them; but the traveler, who best described them, was Norden, who gave a minute description. They existed then amid the ruins of an edifice, made of marble, granite, and verd-antique, supposed to be either the palace of Alexander, an edifice erected by the Ptolemies, or the palace of Cæsar. The obelisks, popularly attributed to Cleopatra, and called her needles, were, however, not erected by Cleopatra, but in the reign of Augustus, in his seventh year, B.C. 24–23, reckoning the first Egyptian regnal year B.C. 30, in which Cleopatra died. This appears from the inscription, found by Mr. Dixon on the bronze crab or scorpion, placed under the erect obelisk, four of which supported it upon its base. They had been already seen, but not perfectly recognized, by the Baron de Tott. The four sides of the obelisk nearly faced to the points of the compass, and, from the construction of the pavement, the lines discovered by Mr. Dixon show, that they had been used as gnomons. A concave dial, also, with Greek ciphers, not earlier than Augustus, was found at the base of one of the Alexandrian obelisks, and presented in 1852 by Mr. J.

Scott Tucker to the British Museum. There is some discrepancy between the inscriptions on the north and west sides, as given by Norden and others. It seems that these two sides, which are turned toward the Mediterranean, are the most destroyed by sea-air. The inscriptions on the more perfect sides have been repeatedly published by Kircher, in the "Description de l'Égypte," and Champollion in his "Monuments." The most complete copy, however, is that supplied in Burton's "Excerpta," pl. lii., which gives the four sides, and has been collated with the others.

The pyramidion on the first side has the following representation: On the right side is Thothmes III., represented as a sphinx, seated on a pylon or pedestal, the same as forms the so-called standard, facing to the right. In both hands he holds a jar of wine, and the inscription on the pedestal calls him "the powerful bull, crowned in the city of Western Thebes, the son of the Sun, Tahutimes (Thothmes)," and in the area is "makes a gift of wine." Before him is the god Ra, Helios, or the Sun, hawk-headed, wearing a disk, seated on a throne, holding a dog-headed sceptre in his right hand and an emblem of life in his left. Ra faces to the left hand. Above their heads is "Haremakhu [Harmachis, a form of Horus, or the sun on the horizon], the great god, lord of the heaven," which is followed by "he [Harmachis] gives all life to the good god, the lord of the two countries, Menkheper-ra [Thothmes III.]."

Each side of this obelisk is decorated with three perpendicular lines of hieroglyphs, the central one on each side being that of Thothmes III., who first set up the obelisk at Heliopolis. The side lines, those to the right and left, were added by Rameses II. of the nineteenth dynasty, the supposed Sesostris, but how or when does not appear—probably they were placed upon it before it was erected; and the monument may have been left unfinished at the death of Thothmes III., and completed long after by his successor, or the lateral lines may have been placed on the monument long after its erection, and when upright, by placing a

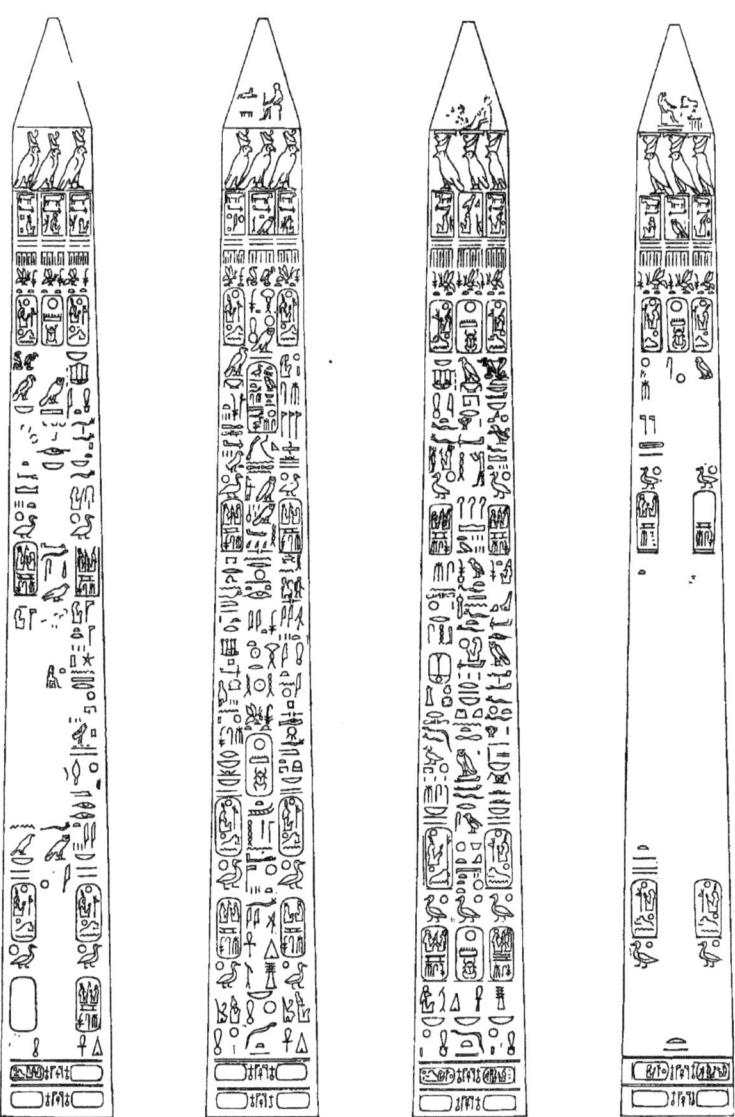

The Hieroglyphs on the four sides of the New York Obelisk.
(From Champollion.)

scaffolding around it, on which the masons stood and worked.

Central line.

The Horus, the powerful bull, crowned in Western Thebes, the lord of diadems, whose kingdom is as extensive as the Sun's in heaven. Tum, the lord of Heliopolis, the son of his race, he has caused him to be born, Tahutimes [Thothmes III.]. They [the gods] made him a great abode in their own beauty, knowing what should be, that he should make his dominion extend as the Sun for ages, the king of Upper and Lower Egypt, Men-kheper-ra [Thothmes III.], beloved of Tum, the great god, and his circle of the gods, giver of all life, stability, and power, like the Sun for ever.

Right line.

The Horus, the powerful bull, beloved of Ra, king of Upper and Lower Egypt, Usermara, approved of the Sun, the Sun produced by the gods, holding the two countries, son of the Sun, Ramessu [II.], beloved of Amen, the beautiful youth much beloved, like the disk of the sun gleaming from the horizon, lord of the two countries, Usermara, approved of the Sun, son of the Sun, Ramessu [II.], beloved of Amen, glory of Tum, giver of life.

Left line.

The Horus, the powerful bull, son of Kheper [a form of Ra], the king of Upper and Lower Egypt, Usermara, approved of the Sun, the golden hawk, rich in years, greatest of the powerful, son of the Sun, Ramessu [II.], beloved of Amen, he has proceeded from the body [of the Sun] to take the diadems, to be the sole lord, the lord of the two countries, Usermara, approved of the Sun, glory of Tum, like the Sun.

In this inscription, as in the others, the last words of each line read, " Giver of eternal life, like the Sun." There are two horizontal lines at the base, titles of Rameses II. This side has, in smaller characters, "King of Upper and Lower Egypt, Kherp-kheper-ra, approved of the Sun, son of the Sun, Uasarkan [I.]," or else of Seti II. At least, so I restore it.

The second side, like the first, has:

Central line.

The Horus, rejoicing in the crown of Upper Egypt, beloved of the Sun, king of Upper and Lower Egypt, Menkheper-ra, the golden hawk, delighting in power, striker of the rulers of foreign lands, taking them, as his father, Ra [the Sun] has ordered him power over all lands, his scimitar victorious by the power of his hands, enlarging the frontiers of Egypt, son of the Sun, Thothmes [III.], giver of life, like the Sun, lord immortal.

Left line.

The Horus, the mighty bull, beloved of Truth, king of Upper and Lower Egypt, lord of festivals of thirty years, like his father, Ptah Tatanen, son of the Sun, Ramessu [II.], beloved of Amen, the Sun produced him to make festivals in Annu [the Heliopolis] to supply the temples, he produced him lord of the two countries, Usermara, son of the Sun, Ramessu [II.], beloved of Amen, all health and life, like the Sun.

Right line.

The mighty bull, son of Tatanen, the king of Upper and Lower Egypt, Usermara, approved of the Sun, the lord of diadems, ruler of Egypt, chastiser of foreign lands, son of the Sun, Ramessu [II.], beloved of Amen, the monarch victorious by his hands in every land, taking the whole of every land, the lord of the two countries, the son of the Sun, Ramessu [II.], beloved of Amen, life, health, and strength, like the Sun.

There is on this side "Kherp-kheper-ra, approved of the Sun, son of the Sun, Uasarkan [I.]."

Third side, pyramidion as before. Thothmes III., as a sphinx, to the right on a pylon; on the left, Tum, seated on a throne, holding sceptre and life; on the pedestal of sphinx, titles of Thothmes III. as before. In the area is "gives a gift" of wine or milk. Above their heads, "Tum, lord of Heliopolis, great god, lord of heaven;" and again, over the king, "The good god, ruler of Heliopolis, king of Upper and Lower Egypt, Men-kheper-ra [Thothmes III.]."

Central line.

The Horus, the mighty bull, crowned in the Thebaid, has adorned the house of the Sun [Ra], embellishing with the beauties of the disk of the Sun Heliopolis, done for the first time in . . . .

Left line.

The Horus, the mighty bull, beloved of Ra, king of Upper and Lower Egypt, Usermara, approved of the Sun, Sun produced by the gods holding the world, Ramessu [IL] beloved of Amen, beloved . . . . never was done the like . . . . Heliopolis, he has set up his memorial before Atum, lord of two countries, Usermara, approved of the Sun, son [of the Sun, Ramessu IL, beloved of Amen], giver of life.

Right line.

The Horus, the mighty bull, son of Ra [the Sun], the king of Upper and Lower Egypt, the golden hawk, rich in years, greatest of the powerful, son of the Sun, Ramessu [IL], beloved of Amen . . . . lord of the two countries, Usermara, son of the Sun, Ramessu [IL], beloved of Amen, like the Sun.

At the base two lines as before. There is the same prenomen of Uasarkan I. at the base here.

The fourth side is also much mutilated.

Central line.

The Horus, the mighty bull, beloved of the Sun, king of Upper and Lower Egypt, Men-kheper-ra . . . .

Right line.

The Horus, the mighty bull, beloved of Truth, Usermara, lord of festivals of thirty years, like his father Ptah, lord of Truth [or Tatanen], son of the Sun, Ramessu [IL], beloved of Amen, god of gods, star of the two worlds at . . . . sun . . . . house . . . . in what is done lord of the two worlds, Usermara, approved of the Sun, son of the Sun, Ramessu [IL], beloved of Amen.

Left line.

Almost wholly illegible.

[. . . . Userma]ra, approved of the Sun . . . . all . . . . son of the Sun, Ramessu, beloved of Amen . . . . lord of the two countries [Usermara, approved of the Sun, son of the Sun, Ramessu IL, beloved of Amen], like the Sun.

Round the base two lines, with titles of Rameses II., as before.

S. BIRCH.

THE OBELISK, ERECTED BY THOTHMES III., KING OF EGYPT.

> THIS old, time-honored monument was born
> When first mechanic lights began to dawn—
> When art was in its cradle; all was done
> By strength of men—and yet great ends were won.
> The shaft up-pointing to the sun, we read
> As meant to show an early simple creed:
> "Sun worship" was the order of that day;
> And time was marked, where shadows round it lay.
> Four thousand years have passed, since it was young
> And raised its head, and far its shadows flung.
> It was rose-tinted, brought from far Syene;
> But it has faded, as though born of men;
> The blushing color of its youth has passed,
> And, like its betters, it is gray at last.

THE OBELISK AND FREEMASONRY.

This granite poem is too long to read ;—
But it evokes a pause—Time's rushing speed,
Whirling its fire-brands in the startled air,
Looks like one ring of light ;—events were there
That fashioned after times : It witnessed all—
Bleared tales of olden times it will recall
By its rude beauty ; hieroglyphics, traced
Upon its surface, years leave undefaced,
Telling the pride of kings, the name and age,—
And *nothing further* shows that opened page.

Raised by a king, its graceful, tapering height
Stood tall and fair in Egypt's sunny light ;
No poem ever penned could e'er display
Such strange adventures as have marked its way :
At first it graced the "*city of the sun ;*"
After a time a higher place it won ;
For great Augustus moved it to the sea,
The pride of a commercial port to be.
Men worshiped it, called it a holy one ;
It stood before their Temple of the Sun.
And, when grown old, it, of the past, proclaimed
The glories for which Egypt had been famed.
Such times have all passed by—upon the strand
It now lies prone—bound for a foreign land.

It was twin-born—its brother shaft now stands
Upon the banks of Thames ; to kindred lands—
To young America this takes its way.
May soft south winds along its passage play ;
It yet may grace fair places—and may see,
For the first time, a people who are free.

CHAPTER II.

FREEMASONRY OLDER THAN OBELISKS AND PYRAMIDS.

AFTER giving these details concerning the *Thothmes' obelisk* and the Masonic signs, emblems, and symbols, discovered thereon by Commander Gorringe, Grand Master Zola, and Consul-General Farman, we shall endeavor to endorse these Masonic tokens by what Mr. and Mrs. Belzoni thought, said, and wrote about ancient Egyptian Masonry as they saw it on the walls and monuments. It may not have been exactly the same, but analogous, as may be realized by these colored and plain illustrations, representing *initiations* on the walls of the different Mystery Chambers in the splendid rock-excavated Masonic Temple, constructed by Pharaoh Seti I. (*Osymandias*) and his son, Rameses II. (*Sesostris*).

The descriptions that accompany the illustrations are opinions Mr. and Mrs. Belzoni formed during and after their sojourn in Egypt. As Egyptology was in its infancy, and little or nothing was known of hieroglyphic deciphering till about 1825, their ideas can hardly agree with Egyptology of 1880.

THE BELZONI MANUSCRIPTS AND ILLUSTRATIONS OF FREEMASONRY.

DEDICATED TO THE MASONIC BRETHREN UNIVERSALLY.

Wisdom was never more exemplified than when it adopted the Pyramidic and Triangular Form of the sublime Architecture of the Heavens, machined on the firm basis of Eternal Stability.

The united Brethren universally will adopt, I hope, the

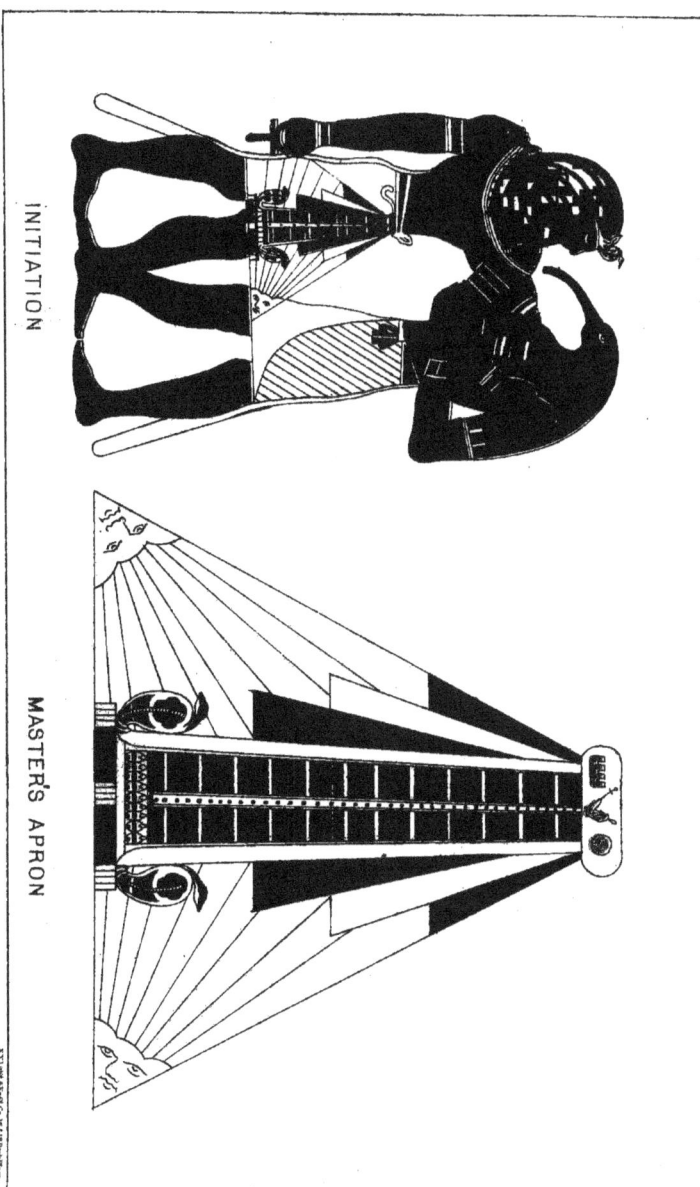

original form of the Masonic Aprons, and establish a jubilee to commemorate the restoration of that event by casting into the flames the present aprons of the unmeaning form of Saint Crispin.

The plate represents Pharaoh Ousirei, King of Egypt, in Masonic communication with one of that order, whose head is covered with a mask, representing the head of the Ibis—an excellent mode of mystifying. The King is invested with the triangular Masonic Apron, holding in his right hand the grand Masonic emblem and last grade obtained.

The second drawing represents the triangular Masonic Apron,* united with the Apron of Serpents.

Masonic signs and signals originated in the first separation that took place in the family of Adam.

From the beginning, Cain and his families had ruled with a despotic power over the numerous families of the passive Adam.

The Elders and Chiefs had been long looking forward for a propitious moment to overthrow the tyrannic power to which they had so long been subjected.

The moment so anxiously hoped for arrived but too soon in the murder of Abel—alas! Abel, son of their hopes, in whom they looked for the fulfilment of the promise, destroyed by his brother, the first-born son of their affliction.

From that period discord entered, with all its train of evils, into the hearts of the human race. A horrible crime had been committed—a dreadful precedent for the unruly and rebellious spirits.

No man felt himself secure from the jealous vengeance of a brother.

Suspicion lurked in each eye. Councils were held by the chiefs of the families, and it was decided that Cain, with

---

* The cartouche in the apron of the Pharaoh in this plate has been translated Rameses II., and not Osiris [see p. 48, also see colored apron.]

his families, should separate and establish themselves at a certain distance from that of Adam.

Well might the afflicted fratricide exclaim, 'My punishment is greater than I can bear!'

The murder of Abel was followed by many important events and inventions of necessity, and many things of serious import to the human race were to be arranged previous to the first separation.

From that catastrophe originated the first civil and moral laws, established for the general protection. And it was enacted that disobedience to those laws and regulations was to be punished by death.

It was a fearful and momentous epoch to the family of Adam. Consultations were held among the chiefs, and great must have been their perplexity to invent and arrange a code of signs and signals that the direct descent of each family from Adam might be known to the others in their future wanderings over the globe.

Independent of the general signals, the heads and chiefs invented private signs, sacred among themselves, for a greater security and brotherly love.

Likewise, each tribe was invested with a standard or banners, as a distinctive attribute, representing certain favorite animals, birds, etc., stuffed, and erected on a tree, to be either carried before them or planted in their encampment.

Civil and religious laws, signs and signals, standards and banners, were the very first inventions of necessity.

The serpent was the grand standard, attached to the family of Abel, or that of Seth, who was invested with universal sovereignty, and to whom was given the birthright of Cain, forfeited by the murder of Abel, and in whose family the priestly and monarchical characters were afterward blended.

In the course of time, as religion increased, the serpent was sanctified and adopted as the armorial and sacred emblematic banner of the monarchic and priestly government united.

THE OBELISK AND FREEMASONRY. 39

The mark set upon Cain and his tribes by which they were to be known to their brethren was, no doubt, represented by or on their banners.

The serpent has ever been held by the ancients as the Grand Mystic Emblem of Paradise Lost, and was the first hieroglyphic emblematic device, and descended from Seth to the families of Ham and to the kings of Egypt, to be traced in the tombs of that wonderful race.

The serpent, united with other devices, was the mystic emblem of the tribes of the human race, and spread universally over the known parts of the globe.

THE ROYAL EGYPTIAN MASONIC APRONS.

Freemasonry commenced from the Creation, and was established by the family of Seth.

The Masonic Apron originated from the covering or apron of fig-leaves, adopted by Adam and Eve after the fall, particularly the Mystic Apron of Serpents, which was dedicated as a memorial to commemorate that fatal event.

The triangular form of the Royal Egyptian Masonic Apron is Masonic, astronomic, and emblematic.

The sun, emblazoned in the corner, spreads its refulgent rays of Divine heat and light over the globe.

The king is never represented in this apron alone. It is accompanied always with the Mystic Apron of Serpents, emblematic of the evil spirit, under the guise of the serpent, that beguiled our fair mother Eve.

The Apron of Serpents is worn alone on State affairs, emblem of the Royal Dynasty and symbol of the fall.

The Triangular Apron I consider as a royal order of the pyramid, to commemorate the occasion for its construction, etc.

The Triangular and Serpent Aprons are exclusively royal. The two aprons appear to have been worn together only on grand Masonic meetings of the hierarchy, whose Lodge was in the sacred recesses of a royal tomb—a solemn type of that death, denounced on the human race by the wilful transgression of the unborn pair.

A finer emblem could not have been adopted to commemorate that mystic and awful event entailed on their posterity until the final conflagration.

Masonry may be traced in all mythology to the remotest parts of the globe.

In the Temples of the Sun and Moon, and in the very Idols of Mexico, in the Pyramids, Tombs, Babel, Stonehenge, and in the Solemn Groves of the Druids.

Masonry shall be traced wherever man is found.

Let the Masonic brethren search, and they will find, that the Egyptian Masonic Key will unlock the hitherto unrevealed mysteries of Egyptian wisdom.

THE TOMB* OF PHARAOH OUSIREI, KING OF EGYPT, IN THE VAL BE-BAN EL MALOOK, THEBES, UPPER EGYPT.

FROM HISTORIC RECORDS SIXTEEN HUNDRED YEARS BEFORE OUR EPOCH.

This tomb was the largest and the last of the tombs discovered by the sacrificed traveler, Giovani Batista Belzoni, in 1818.

The above tomb was dedicated to the Masonic Mysteries, blended and united with emblems of discoveries, inventions, and sciences in general, progressively, as they took place after the Creation, from which originated the many fabulous inventions, with which mythology teems.

Freemasonry in the earlier ages was very different from what is now denominated by that appellation, and, at the epoch of the above tomb, had attained a grandeur and sublimity unknown in Europe.

Pharaoh Ousirei, King of Egypt, is represented in the greater part of this tomb, as going through the ceremonies of initiation into the sublime mysteries of Masonry, etc.

From hieroglyphic drawings in the said tomb, there ap-

---

* Rather Masonic Temple of Pharaohs Seti I. and Rameses II.

THE OBELISK AND FREEMASONRY. 41

pear to be represented three distinct epochs in the life of the young king.

First, on his accession to the kingdom, we behold him going through certain forms and ceremonies, receiving instructions from the hierarchy in the science and secret art of governing.

Having passed his inauguration and being accepted by the sacred order, I now introduce my young king, established, I hope, in all his royal prerogatives.

BELZONI'S ATLAS.

Plate first represents the king, seated on his throne, with the Mystic Apron of Serpents, emblem of royalty, and symbol of the fall.

A sceptre in his hand and incense burning before him.

The first four hieroglyphics at the back of the eagles are Masonic.*

Plate second: The Arms of the Nation, blended with the name of the king's dynasty, offerings, etc.

The spread eagle above, with an ostrich feather in each claw, an eagle at each side as supporters, holding forth the Grand Emblem of Masonry, with armorial bearings, Grades in Masonry, etc., which forms the three eagles.

Plate third: The Royal Name, with winged supporters on each side, holding the Grand Emblem, the name orna-

---
* See the translation of these hieroglyphs, p. 50.

mented with globes and feathers, figures kneeling on splendid cushions.

Plate fourth: Passing certain Mystic Grades, etc.

Plate nineteenth:* The High Priest, Grand Master, or High Grand Master, represented in a Temple, seated on a throne of state, supported on a platform; around the base of the platform, are the Masonic hieroglyphics, emblems of stability, power, etc., surmounted by winged globes, etc., a Serpent attached to it, emblematic of its direful influence over it.

A beautiful emblematic border of serpents and globes crowns the whole.

The Winged Globe is accompanied by the following inscription, according to Dr. Young:

"The sacred Father of the protecting powers:
"Living, unalterable, reigning, ministering."

In the above Temple the king is presented to the High Grand Master by one of that order; his head covered with a mask representing the head of a hawk, denoting his descent, rank, and order, grade, etc., with his right hand griping the right shoulder of the king, holding in his left the Masonic Key.

The Female at the side of the Grand Master is one belonging to the hierarchy, she holds the key without the knowledge of its mysterious virtues.

That females were permitted to assist in certain outward forms and ceremonies, processions, etc., is clearly evident.

The king, having gone through the whole of the Mystic Science, we pass with His Majesty into the Masonic Hall of Beauties where His Majesty is accompanied by the Masonic Order, and receives the last and highest grade in Masonry.

---

* See Plate 19, p. 46.

THE MASONIC KEY.*

In this hall the king is invested with the Triangular Masonic Apron.

In the same hall the king is represented in the act of offering costly vases of perfumed ointments to the female aristocracy, there assembled to honor the occasion.

The king is then divested of the Triangular and Serpent Aprons, while presenting the offerings to the females.

ON THE ORIGIN OF THE LEVEL AND PERPENDICULAR.†

The Level was first employed in the erection of Babylon. From its discovery proceeded the word Freemason, unknown until some time after the dispersion at Babel.

Nimrod, the royal and mighty hunter, who with his vast tribes, had long been masters of the Land of Shinar, united with the royal herdsman Asshur and his tribes in the strongest bonds of friendship. Esau was a hunter and Jacob a shepherd.

The two occupations of hunter and shepherd were from the beginning inseparable, and generally of the same family. The protection of the hunters was necessary to guard the flocks against beasts of prey, etc.

Nimrod and Asshur appear from Scripture authority to have been two of the most powerful princes among the unsettled nations; their occupations rendered them of the utmost consequence to the nations round about; for to them all were tributary.

The confederate princes and sheiks of the unsettled tribes and nations had long contemplated the necessity of a

---

* See translation, p. 50.

† Assyriology and Cuneiform translations are rendering these speculations more probable.

general separation and dispersion over the whole globe, " as the lands could not contain the multitude."

A convention had been entered into by the heads and chiefs of the nations with Nimrod and Asshur, that the united nations should by degrees assemble and encamp on the plains of Shinar for an indefinite period, where councils were to be held among the rulers to take into serious consideration the arrangement of the separation and dispersion.

Nimrod and Asshur undertook to supply the nations with provisions, cattle, beasts of burden, etc. The governments of the nations there assembled agreeing on their part to assist in founding the kingdom of Babylon and Assyria for Nimrod and Asshur, etc. And it was decreed among them that, after Babylon was finished, they should, before separating, assist in erecting a monument, on a scale of gigantic height, as a record to future generations, and to commemorate the name, descent and attributes of each nation assembled there for the express purpose of a general dispersion of the vast multitudes of the younger branches of the family of Noah.

"Let us build us a city and a tower whose top may reach unto heaven; let us make us a name lest we be scattered abroad upon the face of the whole earth."

These words alone prove that the plan for building the tower was that of the perpendicular instead of the pyramidal and tent form, which cannot appear very high, because its height is lost in the great expanse; and this is what disappoints the travelers at the first view of the Pyramids. The wonderful rapidity with which the kingdoms had been raised, with the aid of the level and the perpendicular, had caused a great sensation among the rulers of the nations, who were each anxious to obtain this invaluable secret. Every stratagem had hitherto been practised to discover it without effect. A few of the chiefs entered into a conspiracy in order to obtain the knowledge of the level and perpendicular, but deferred it until the Tower of Babel should have attained a certain height, when they would suspend their work.

All had gone on in perfect harmony, and all were anxious to evince their zeal in this brotherly undertaking, when, alas! " trifles light as air " began to assume a form of hostility. None but those forming the conspiracy were aware of what was intended, yet all felt that some threatened mischief was at hand.

Jealousy broke forth in all its horrors, and all was anarchy and confusion that destroyed the well-laid plans, which had taken many years to arrange in regular order for the separation, when the royal and noble associates in architecture and the discoverers of the greatest discovery ever made in science—namely, the level and perpendicular mode of building—were obliged to flee from the fury of malignant jealousy, in order to retain their secret and their lives.

They fled, no doubt, to the nations established by Mizraim, where such talents were sure to be received with royal honors.

And to the confusion which took place at Babel are we indebted for the first perpendicular temples in Egypt.

The noble associates had bought their experience dearly, and in order to prevent the monster jealousy from interfering with their grand secret, they consulted with the royal and noble of each nation, from which consultation a society was formed of the most learned men, who were initiated into the secret of the perpendicular, etc.

Each royal and noble initiate kept a retinue of workers of his own. None were permitted to build who were not of that society. They traveled in royal style, and each nation they visited added its strength, stability, and power to that fraternity.

Signs and signals were invented, so that the initiated were known to each other in all lands. Those associations were denominated Royal Freemasons.

The drawings in the tomb of Pharaoh Ousirei prove

46   THE OBELISK AND FREEMASONRY.

that Freemasonry, from the creation and after the confusion of Babel, was perfectly conservative.

SARAH BELZONI.

BRUSSELS, Oct., 1843.

"O happy, blessed is he that witnesseth the initiation of the deities; for he venerateth the source of life."—EURIPIDES: *Bacchæ*, 73.

The Belzoni manuscripts say so little about the 19th Plate of Belzoni's Atlas, that we cannot help giving it here by itself and saying, that it speaks for itself, and no Mason can look at the attitudes of this group of Grand Master, Guide, Candidate, and Assistant, without realizing that, if there are Masonic institutions now, there were similar, if not identical ones, about four thousand years ago, in the land of the Pharaohs, and that modern Freemasonry had its prototype in the Masonic Temple of Seti I. and Rameses II, where applicants were initiated as Oriental and Occidental Masonic orders initiate now. Throughout the thirteen highly ornamented mystery chambers of the Seti and Rameses temple are nine different initiations, little differing from those we give in this epitome. The position of the hands of the Grand Master here, the right hand of the guide and candidate, as well as the posture of the assistant, look like an initiation to some Masonic degree. In vain will some Masons say these performances belonged to Egyptian religious mysteries. No one but such as have not attentively looked at them will talk of religious rites and ceremonies. The attitudes, eyes, and faces of the individuals, the signs, emblems, and symbols around them, indicate anything but religion or devotion. There is nothing humble, devotional, or prayerful in their countenances or in their postures. The four or five initiatory groupings in the preceding ninth and tenth mystery chambers seem to indicate no religion. The last one, where the candidate comes before the Grand Master with raised hands, is so well known to Masons that it needs no explanation. Any brother who will take the trouble to go and see the beautiful illustrations of Belzoni's discoveries at the Astor Library, or come and look over the series presented to us by Mrs. Belzoni, may realize that the groupings and their surroundings were purely Masonic.

CHAPTER III.

"Many thousand pilgrims of all nations, etc., will succeed us—ascend these pyramids, and contemplate them with astonishment."—LEPSIUS.

As so much has been discovered in Egypt, and translated from hieroglyphs, since Mr. and Mrs. Belzoni conceived and wrote the preceding pages, we add the following data:

The three hieroglyphs in the *cartouche* of Rameses' *Masonic Apron* had ever attracted our attention. Now is the occasion to decipher them, if possible. While consulting English, French, and German authorities on the subject, we found in the recent works of Mariette, Chabas, and Pierret, that phonetically the three hieroglyphs, sounded in ancient Egyptian *Ra*,* *Ma*,† *Setp*,‡ meant, "*The chosen of the Sun and Truth.*" The first time we showed this cartouche to the veteran Egyptologist, Seyffarth, he said it was the titular name of Rameses the Great. The second time he saw it he pronounced it the titular name of Osymandias, which seemed a contradiction; but Mariette, in his treatise on Abydos, explains this discrepancy when he tells us that Rameses II. only bore a part of the titular name during the life of his father, Seti I., or Menephtah,

Ra, god of the Sun; †*Ma*, goddess of Truth and Justice; ‡*Setp*, chosen or elect. Out of these monosyllabic words subsequent dialects and languages have made *Rameses*, which clearly shows that vowel sounds change, whereas consonant sounds remain. Thus, consonants are bricks, and vowels mortar; hence, the ancients only wrote the consonants.

MYSTERY CHAMBER Nº 9.

called Osymandias by the Greeks, and only assumed the full titular name after Seti's death. Hence, we realize that Rameses the Great, styled Sesostris by the Greeks, and his father, Osymandias, who jointly reigned over fifty years, bore the same titular name, meaning, " *Chosen of the Sun and Ma ;* but, phonetically and literally, it was *Ra-Ma-Setp,* from which was formed Rameses. Maspéro, in his " Histoire Ancienne des Peuples de l'Orient," p. 227, corroborates Mariette, Chabas, and Pierret, as to the titular name of Rameses II. Thus did *Rameses,* with the three consonants, R, M, S, the very frame of the ancient Egyptian name, reach us from and through ancient Egyptian or Coptic, Hebrew, Greek, and Latin, into which Moses, the Seventy, and St. Jerome, translated it from Egyptian.

The veteran Egyptologist Seyffarth agrees with me, that the third hieroglyph has not been clearly copied, but it must mean *chosen, elect,* or *beloved,* in this connection.

[NOTE.—The word *Rameses* came to us as the name of a land, and as the name of a city; for we read in the Mosaic account, Gen. 47: 11: "Joseph placed his father and brethren, and gave them a possession in the land of Egypt, in the best land, in the *land of Rameses,* as Pharaoh had commanded." Was this land called after some Pharaoh, or was some Pharaoh called after this best land in Egypt?

Next we find, Ex. 1: 11: "Therefore, they did set over them task-masters to afflict them with their burdens, and they built for Pharaoh treasure-cities Pithom and *Raamses.*" As to the site of this famous treasure-city, Brugsch, Chabas, and other Egyptologists, tell us it was built by the Israelites, under taskmasters, in the land of *Rameses,* given them by Joseph. Brugsch thinks it was *Tanis,* and Chabas says it was *Pelusium.*

Again we read, Ex. 12: 37: "The children of Israel journeyed from *Rameses* to Succoth, about six hundred thousand on foot that were men, besides children."

Moses gives this event more detailed, Num. 33: 3-5:

"They departed from *Rameses* in the first month, on the fifteenth day of the first month; on the morrow after the Passover the children of Israel went out with a high hand in the sight of all the Egyptians.

"And the children of Israel removed from *Rameses*, and pitched in Succoth."

Recent hieroglyphic translations concerning prisoners under taskmasters during the reign of Rameses II. (*Sesostris*), who issued a decree forbidding his officials to give the prisoners straw to make bricks; and bricks having been found lately in the country where the Israelites dwelt, has awakened discussion among Egyptologists and commentators. Hieroglyphic translations, monuments, and ruins, may yet furnish clear data concerning the Israelites, their position in Egypt, and their exodus.

Concerning the four hieroglyphs in the Belzoni manuscripts, p. 41, I went to the venerable octogenarian Egyptologist, Seyffarth, to ask him for his hieroglyphic key, in order to translate them. He kindly got his key, showed me the hieroglyph on the right,* and said it means *sceptre*. Then he turned to the second, saying it signifies *atlas*, the third *brain*, and the fourth *sick*. Hence, their meaning is *sceptre, atlas, brain, sick*.

I asked whether atlas here means ancient Mount *Atlas*, to which he answered no; but it signifies *atlas* in the spine. I told him then *atlas* here must rather have a symbolic sense. He observed Latin *firmare* (establish) would probably render the sense here; but these hieroglyphs cannot be properly translated, unless they stand in the original connection, where they were used. Next we talked about the hieroglyphs in the cartouche of the Rameses apron. On my way home I thought of the connections, and came to the conclusion that it was part of a charge or address to Prince Rameses, who was to succeed his father, Seti I., in which connection it

---

* The Egyptians, like most Oriental races, wrote and read from right to left, omitting vowels.

rationally means, "The sceptre establishes or renders the brain sick," or, better, "*The sceptre addles the brain.*"

Another hieroglyph in the Belzoni MS., p. 43, is called *Masonic key*. As it occurs among the four just translated, and means *brain, intellect*, etc., we may consider it as translated. It seems to have been a mark of royalty in Egypt. It was considered as a symbol of immortality. It is called "*crux ansata*" and *Tau*. It was a symbol in Assyria, Egypt, and India. It is also a symbol in high Masonic degrees. It has a deep esoteric meaning, which the ancients perceived in the ever reproductive principles of Nature. Some of our scientists style these principles *Cosmic forces;* some *male* and *female* principle; and others call them *positive* and *negative*, especially since the power of *magnetism* and *electricity* has become better known.]

CHAPTER IV.

PENTAOUR, EPIC ON THE BATTLE OF KADESH.

CONNECTED with Pharaoh Rameses II. (Sesostris), founder of the magnificent rock-excavated Masonic Temple, is the earliest epic poem extant, called *Pentaour*, which we cannot help translating here from " Histoire Ancienne des Peuples de l'Orient " (pp. 227–232), by G. Maspéro,* Prof. of the Egyptian Language and Archeology in the College of France. This poem is inscribed on the walls of the Temple of Karnak in hieroglyphs. It seems Rameses II. had a Poet Laureate, called *Pentaour*, who composed this ancient epic on the Battle of Kadesh,† where the Kheta ‡ and their numerous Asiatic allies lay in ambush for the youthful Egyptian king, who, surrounded by his opponents, penetrated the ranks of the perverse Kheta. He was alone, no other with him, having thus advanced within sight of those who were behind himself, in the midst of all the warriors of the perverse Kheta and the numerous nations who accompanied them—the people of Aradus, of Mysia, of Pedasa.

---

* Maspéro tells us (pp. 231 and 232) the translation into French is from the Papyrus Raifé and Sallier by M. de Rougé, Prof. of Egyptology in the College of France, 1856. No doubt, Maspéro knows about the version of Pentaour by Goodwin and Lushington.

† Kadesh or Kades, a city on the river Orontes, in Syria.

‡ Perhaps of the race of Σκυθαι, *Scythæ*, *Scythians*, *Getæ*, who dwelled in Asiatic and European Scythia, Armenia, Assyria, Media, Asia Minor, Syria, Phenicia, and Palestine, where a city was called after them Scythopolis, and where, according to Herod (B. IV., 6 and 7; B. I., 106), they ruled twenty-eight years. Also the *Khatti* of Assyria and the *Katti* of Germany (Tacitus: Ann. B., II., 7) may have been of the same stock; so may have been Homer's *Keteioi*.

Each of their chariots carried three men, and they were united. The Pharaonic poet thus describes the deeds of his youthful hero: "No prince was with me! no general, no officer of the archers or chariots. My soldiers have abandoned me; my cavaliers have fled before them, and not one has remained to fight near me. Who art Thou, then? O my Father, Ammon! Does a father forget his son? Have I ever done anything without thee? Have I not advanced and stopped at thy command? I have not violated thy orders. He is great, the lord of Egypt, who overturns the barbarians in his way! What are these Asiatics before thee? Ammon, enervate those infidels. Have I not made innumerable offerings to thee? I filled thy sacred temples with prisoners; I built to thee a temple for millions of years; I have given thee all my riches for thy magazines; I have offered thee the entire world to enrich thy domain. . . . . Surely, a miserable fate awaits any one, who opposes thy designs! Happiness to any one, who knows thee; for thy deeds proceed from a heart full of love. I invoke thee, O my Father, Ammon! Behold me in the midst of numerous nations, unknown to me; all nations are united against me, and I am alone, no other with me. My numerous soldiers have abandoned me; none of my cavaliers looked toward me; when I called them not one of them listened to my voice; but I think Ammon is worth more to me than a million of soldiers, than a hundred thousand cavaliers, than a myriad of brothers or young sons, even if they were all united together! The work of men is nothing; Ammon will conquer and carry the day. I accomplished these things by the counsel from thy mouth. O Ammon, I have not transgressed thy command! Behold, I have rendered glory unto thee to the extremities of the earth!

"The voice has resounded as far as Hermonthis. Ammon listens to my invocation; he gives me his hand. I utter a cry of joy, he speaks behind me: 'I hasten to thee, to thee, Rameses Meiamun. . . . . I am with thee. It is I, thy father! My hand is with thee, and I am worth more than hundreds of thousands. I am the Lord of strength, loving valor. I have found a courageous heart, and I am satisfied. My will shall be done.'

"Like unto Month, I thrust my arrows right and left, and overturn the enemies. I am like Baal, in his hour, before them. The two thousand five hundred chariots, that surround me, are broken into pieces before my steeds. Not one of them finds a hand to fight; the heart fails in their breast, and fear enervates their limbs. They no longer know how to throw their darts, and find no strength to hold their lances. I throw them into the waters as the crocodile falls into them. They are lying on their faces, one above the other, and I kill in the midst of them. I desire not one shall look behind himself and none shall return; he who falls shall not rise again.

"The prince of Kheta, triumphant as he appeared, felt himself suddenly stopped in the midst of his victory by an invisible power, and recoiled, struck with terror, etc., and all efforts were vain. I thrust myself among them like Month; my hand devoured them in an instant; I killed and massacred in the midst of them. They said to each other: 'This is not a man who is among us, it is Sutekh, the great warrior; it is Baal in person. These are not the deeds of a man. Alone, all alone, he repels hundreds of thousands, without leaders and without soldiers. Let us hasten to flee; let us save our lives, and breathe once more the free air.' Whoever came to fight him felt his hand grow weaker; they could no longer hold either bow or lance. Seeing that he had reached the cross-road, the king pursued them like a griffin. . . . . Be firm; steady your hearts, O my soldiers! You see my victory, and I was all alone; it is Ammon, who gave me strength; his hand is with me.

" He encouraged his charioteer, Menna, whom the number of enemies filled with fear, and thrust himself into the thickest of the fight. Six times I charged through the enemies. Finally his army arrived toward evening and extricated him. He assembled his generals and overwhelmed them with reproaches. 'What will the entire world say, when they learn, that you left me alone and without a second? that not a prince, not an officer of chariots or archer joined his hand to mine? I fought, I repulsed millions of people, I alone! Victory of Thebes and Contented Noura were my grand horses; I found them at hand, when I was alone in the midst of shuddering enemies. I shall feed them myself every day, when I shall be in my palace; for I found them, when I was in the midst of my enemies, with Menna, my charioteer, and with the officers of my house, who accompanied me, and were witnesses of the combat. Behold those whom I found. I returned after a victorious struggle, and struck with my sword the assembled multitudes."

Next day the battle was renewed, and the Asiatics were routed. The king of the Kheta sued for peace, which Rameses granted, and triumphantly returned to Egypt.

"Ammon came to salute him, saying: 'Come, our beloved son, O Rameses Meiamun!' The gods gave him infinite periods of eternity on the double throne of his father Atum, and all the nations were thrown under his sandals."

Soon Rameses the Great married the Khetan princess, Ra-ma-ur-nofre (*Sun — Truth — Beautiful exceedingly*), daughter of Khetasar, King of Kheta, who visited Egypt.

The battle, so tersely described in this heroic poem, is grandly illustrated on the pylon and walls of the Rameseum at Luxor, Karnak, and Ipsambul, which clearly shows that it was considered the great event in Egyptian history, and that Egypt had artists to paint and sculpture her heroes and their deeds. No wonder the hierophant of Thebes, who explained the hieroglyphic inscriptions to Germanicus, A.D. 18, said: * "That the whole army was called forth into the field by *Rhamses*, one of the kings of Egypt, and, under the auspices of that monarch, overran all Libya, Ethiopia, and in their progress subdued the Medes and Persians, the Bactrians and Scythians, with the extensive regions inhabited

---

* Tacitus: Ann., B. II., 60.

by the Syrians, the Armenians, and their neighbors, the Cappadocians," etc.

Here we find the conquests of prior Egyptian Pharaohs, like Thothmes, Amenophis, etc., ascribed to the youthful Rameses the Great, whose nine initiations are so artistically illustrated in the rock-excavated subterranean Masonic palace, discovered by Belzoni, accompanied by his faithful helpmeet, Sarah.

Pentaour's heroic essay makes us realize, that Egypt had not only builders of pyramids and obelisks, but conquerors, warriors, scholars, and poets, to record and sing their apotheoses. Moreover, it shows that the ancient Egyptians were a religiously inclined people, and masters in improvising prayers; for even their kings were expected to invoke the Deity before going into battle. No pietist can say, that the ancient idolaters on the Nile did not know how to compose prayers. When the numerous papyri have been translated, they will constitute a rich Egyptian literature in all branches.

The great statesman and classic scholar, Gladstone, while writing his "*Time and Place of Homer*," perceived a point of comparison between Homer's Achilles and Pentaour's Rameses the Great, and justly thought the Greek bard must have heard or read of the exploits of the Egyptian Pharaoh. Hence we read, p. 197, "of the great Egyptian empire of Rameses II. and the Nineteenth Dynasty, Homer, or at least Hellas, may, or rather must, humanly speaking, have known something, on account of their relation to continental and yet more certainly to insular Greece, etc., ... some *tenuis aura*, some breath, at least, of the personal renown of the Egyptian kings and warriors must have passed into the atmosphere of Greece, etc. . . . . According to the Pentaour, this monarch personally performed in the war with the Kheta such prodigies of valor as may fairly be deemed without example, and considered to approximate to the superhuman. Was it the echo of these feats of war, or of this resounding celebration of them, that suggested to Homer the colossal scale of his Achilles?" etc. . . . .

This prelude is followed by a classic research full of archeological and linguistic acumen, and a cogent dissertation on the Iliad and Odyssey. This essay, covering seventy-five highly interesting pages to classic scholars, logically concludes: "Now, not only is it probable that Homer had personal access to these sources, but we may almost say, it is certain. Certain, by reason not solely, nor perhaps mainly, of the activity of his mind and his vast power of appropriation, but also because of his station as a bard."

CHAPTER V.

TOMB OF SETI I., COMMONLY CALLED BELZONI'S TOMB.

PERHAPS our readers would like to know what Mariette Bey, the collector and present directeur of the museum at Cairo, says, in his "*Monuments of Upper Egypt*," p. 235, of the Tomb of Seti I., commonly called Belzoni's Tomb: " This is the most magnificent of all the tombs of Bab-el-Molouk; by its grandeur and the profusion of sculptures with which it is adorned, it eclipses all others, etc. . . . . The visitor, however, will soon perceive to what sad mutilations it has been subjected. Rumor attributes these acts of vandalism to certain explorers of Egypt, etc. . . . . It is more correct to say, that the desecration of one of the most valuable monuments of Egypt is the work of dealers in antiquities, or even of the tourists themselves. The fact is that the latter, in their recklessness, purchase almost at any price relics which, after all, are simply the proceeds of an irreparable wrong done to science.

"Immediately on entering the tomb the visitor finds himself actually transported into a new world, etc. . . . . Even the gods themselves assume strange forms. Long serpents glide hither and thither round the rooms, or stand erect against the doorways. Some malefactors are being decapitated, and others are precipitated into the flames. Well might a visitor feel a kind of horror creeping over him, etc. . . . . The judgment of the soul after being separated from the body, and the many trials, which it will be called upon to overcome by the aid only of such virtues, as it has evinced while on earth, constitute the subject-matter of the almost endless representations, which cover the tomb from the entrance to the extreme end of the last chamber. The serpents standing erect over each portal, darting out venom, are the guardians of the gates of heaven—the soul cannot pass unless justified by works of piety and benevolence.

"The long texts, displayed over other parts of the walls, are magnificent hymns, etc. . . . . When once the dead has been adjudged worthy of life eternal, these ordeals are at an end; he becomes part of the divine essence, and henceforward a pure spirit, he wanders over the vast regions, where the stars forever shine. Thus the tomb is only the emblem of the voyage of the soul to its eternal abode. The soul has no sooner left the body than we are called upon from room to room to witness its progress, as it appears before the gods and becomes gradually purified, until at last, in the grand hall at the end of the tomb we are presented at its final admission into that life, which a second death shall never reach."

It is astonishing the French savant could see nothing but religious ceremonies and performances in the nine distinct initiatory meetings of candidate and master, and in the intermediate persons, attendants, and even horrors, that have ever belonged to some of the Masonic initiations. To consider these attitudes of the Masonic candidate and master as soul and god, must seem strange, if not grotesque, to any Mason who has gone through some of the grand trial grades which include, not only alluring Venus, but utter darkness, solitude, fire, water, knocking in the head, and all the horrors human ingenuity has been able to devise short of real death. It would be much more rational to consider these ordeals and horrors as initiatory Masonic trials, through which the candidate has to pass, before he can reach the grand "*Hall of Beauties*," where triumph crowns all the pangs and sufferings incident to some of the initiations, not even excepting the dark deep well within the vast Masonic palace, wherein was found but one real mummy and a beautiful empty alabaster sarcophagus, as a reminder of real death. To call this a tomb is a misnomer, let who will style it so. No wonder a New York *Herald* reporter asked the French savant, who tried to speak lightly about Freemasonry, "Monsieur Mariette, are you a Mason?" to which the savant replied, "No," and stopped his raillery. An intelligent Mason has but to glance at the attitudes of the Nineteenth Plate in Belzoni's Atlas, and he must realize that the whole scene is a Masonic initiation, and so with those that precede.

Belzoni named the splendid subterranean palace, Tomb of Psammuthis;* but Mariette and other Egyptologists have called it Tomb of Seti I. (Osymandias). As the cartouche of the apron translates: "*Chosen of the Sun and Truth*, syllabically † *Ra-ma-setp* (Rameses), we think the place should be called: *Masonic Temple of Seti I. and Rameses II.*, for wherever we find a full representation of Rameses the Great, whether in Lower, Middle, or Upper Egypt, he wears the Masonic apron, and may therefore be styled the Masonic Pharaoh *par excellence*. No doubt, he figured at all the meetings in that cool and secluded spot as long as he lived. Belzoni found but one mummy and an empty alabaster sarcophagus in that elaborately adorned temple; there is no reason for calling it a tomb, especially when we consider that Death is a requisite in Masonic initiations, and that the mummy and sarcophagus were there for that purpose.

---

* Psammuthis, of the 26th Dynasty, reigned fifteen years at Sais, 603, B. C., whereas Psammuthis of the 29th Dynasty reigned but one year at Mendes, 379, B.C. As the work of that colossal excavation must have required Egypt's most prosperous period and enterprise, it could not have been accomplished as late as 603 or 379, B.C., and during short reigns of one or fifteen years. Only the long and glorious rule of sixty years under Osymandias and his son Sesostris (Rameses II.) suit such a herculean task.

† Thus Seyffarth's syllabic key for translating hieroglyphs has been, is, and will be, rendering Egyptian literature more and more accessible, so that we shall be able to throw light on primitive oriental history, whether in Egypt, Assyria, Canaan, India, Arabia, etc. . . . . which were all more or less connected in remote ages. Cuneiforms are assisting that development.

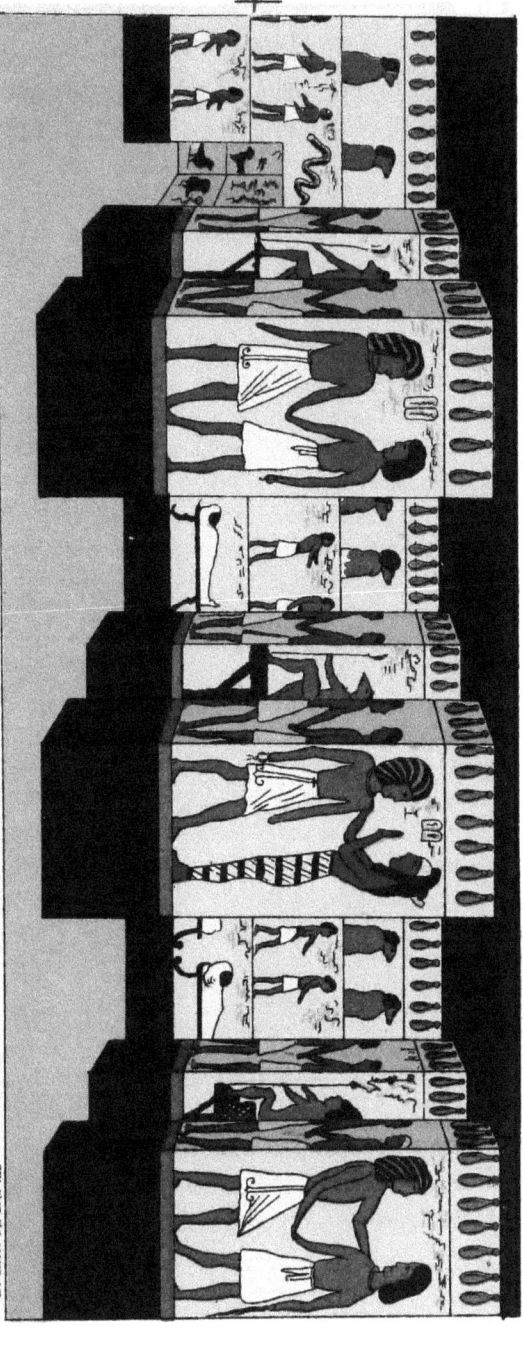

MYSTERY CHAMBER Nº 10.

THE OBELISK AND FREEMASONRY. 61

Amelia B. Edwards, in her "*Thousand Miles up the Nile*," 1877, speaking of a temple in Upper Egypt, says (p. 497), it was "coated as usual with a thin film of stucco, and colored with a richness for which I know no parallel, except in the tomb of Seti L, at Thebes, commonly known as Belzoni's Tomb." We consider it incumbent on Freemasonry all over the world to restore that hallowed spot to its pristine design and make it the *Mecca* of a universal Masonic brotherhood. We have no doubt the present Khedive, who is so liberally inclined, will say: "*So mote it be.*"

As there is now a movement to enable Abraham's long exiled progeny to return to Palestine and restore the Promised Land, why should there not be a simultaneous effort to reinstate the brilliant Masonic Temple, where Rameses the Great was initiated four milleniums ago? Thus the Jews, who have been persecuted for two thousand years by Gentiles and Christians, and the Freemasons, who have been ostracized by Church and State, could sympathize, both having upheld the lamp of art, science, and progress, in the midst of ignorance and superstition.

The Duke of Cyprus, Rothschild, and five millions of Abrahamites, Zola, Grand Master of Egypt, and Dr. Fanton, of Macedonia, recently so conspicuous concerning the Masonic emblems on the American obelisk, the Druses, Grand Orient, Parsees, and especially the Brethren of Ishmael,* might approach the Khedive on the subject; for it seems, from what Mrs. Edwards says, that Belzoni's misnamed tomb looks yet charming, and deserves to be called "*Hall of Beauties*," as it did, when the great explorer, Belzoni, and his intrepid helpmeet, opened it, 1818.

We are sure the Prince of Wales, Grand Master of England, and Premier Gladstone would back the movement with all the prestige of Great Britain. Thus might the torch of recent civilization be carried into retrograded Asia

---

* A powerful order, having members all over the globe, two of whose three chiefs always reside in the orient, and one in the occident.

and Africa, having Gibraltar, Malta, Cyprus, and Aden connected by the Suez Canal, a universal Masonic Temple, near Pharaonic Thebes, a liberalized Jewish empire in Palestine, a vast British empire in India, and progressing Japan in the distant orient, linked to Republican America by steam. Such are the prospects of Freemasonry and Judaism, assisted by the ubiquitous English-speaking populations.

CHAPTER VI.

BELZONI MANUSCRIPTS, DRAWINGS, THE HAND OF A MUMMY, ETC.

As readers may wish to know how, when, and where we obtained the Belzoni manuscripts, drawings, etc., we state the occasion and circumstances:

During my sojourn in Brussels, 1849, I lived in "Madame Belzoni's" house, and became her medical adviser. I frequently conversed with her about her husband's travels and discoveries. She was with Belzoni during his Egyptian explorations, and wrote a graphic "Account of the Women of Egypt, Nubia, and Syria," which is very interesting, showing, as it does, the family relations and private life of the Mahometans. She ascended and descended the Nile, gazed at the Pyramids, and saw the mystic figures and hieroglyphics on the walls of the rock-excavated palaces,. whose analogues, perhaps prototypes, are found at Elephanta, in India.

Among other pleasant recollections of this energetic lady, I cannot help mentioning the delicate manner, in which she presented to me the right hand of a mummy now in the Brussels Museum, minus the hand. It is considered as the hand of an Egyptian queen.

The evening before our departure for America she invited my wife and me to take tea with her. We went with great pleasure; we were the only guests. As she had taken a warm interest in the stirring events of 1848, we conversed freely about them; but archeologic researches, with their kindred sciences and arts, such as ethnology, architecture, etc., were favorite topics with her. She spoke of Mr. Gliddon, whom she saw in Egypt; described her journey through the Holy Land only with a guide; how she accompanied her husband during his arduous labors; but said now she had but one desire, which was to visit America, in order to see Niagara and the Indian Mounds, described by Squier and Davis, and the Central American ruins, so clearly delineated by Stephens. From such conversation on the part of one nearly three score and ten, we may infer that she was still young in mind. Yes, she fully enjoyed and appreciated all that was going on in the world. The interest she took in human affairs had preserved, as it always does, her bodily vigor. I saw her, winter and summer, taking out-door exercise, which gave to her robust and well proportioned frame a healthy and cheerful look. She was English, and earnestly desired her country's welfare; but she did not think, as her countrymen generally do, that there is nothing worth having out of England.

Thus the evening had passed delightfully, and we were about taking leave, when she said, in a most winning tone of voice: "Doctor, will you do me a favor?" "Certainly, Madame, I will do anything in my power for you." "Then you will accept this hand; I have carried it about me for twenty-two years in remembrance of my husband and his discoveries." "Madame, I am the last man to deprive you of so precious a relic." "But you just said you will do anything in your power for me. It is surely in your power to accept it as a memento of me." "As such, Madame, I will gratefully accept and keep it." So I took the hand, together with the writings and drawings, saying: "Madame, will you do me the favor to write something on these papers?" she seized a pen and wrote: "*My Unlettered Theory.*" "Madame, what use do you wish me to make of these articles?" "I give them to you, and leave their use to your own discretion." We took an affectionate leave of one, who had seen the world, with its pleasures and disappointments, and was still willing to perform her part in the great drama.

In 1851 or 1852 Parliament voted to "*Madame Belzoni*"

an annual pension of one hundred pounds sterling, a tardy reward to a daughter worthy of England, and to the widow of an Italian, who had sacrificed his life to advance science, and to enrich the British Museum with rare relics of antiquity.

The good lady needed this help very much; for she told me she had passed twenty-two years in Brussels, during which she had repeatedly petitioned Parliament for a pension, in consideration of her husband's services. To support herself she hired a large house, and underlet the best parts of it. When I became acquainted with her she lived on the upper floor of a house near the "*Boulevard de Waterloo.*" Her only society at home were two small Italian greyhounds, the most intelligent animals I ever saw. They not only understood human language, but even looks and insinuations. I often thought the next appearance in their serial development would be in the shape of bright, intellectual children. She was known all over Brussels as "*Madame Belzoni.*"

I cannot omit here a striking anecdote, that was related to me by this remarkable lady. Such, about, was her language: "In 1823 I was in Paris; I went to bed and fell asleep, but was suddenly awakened by two or three very strong knocks at the head-board of my bed. It immediately flashed upon me, that something must have happened to my husband, who was in Africa, and on his way to Timbuctoo. I saw the curtain of my bed move; I jumped out of bed, thinking I perceived a human figure; I felt as though something were gliding by me. The moon was shining very bright; I searched the room, walked all around the bed, and looked under it, but I saw nothing. I looked at my watch, it was two o'clock. I did not feel like going to sleep again, so I dressed myself, feeling much agitated, and sure that Belzoni was dead. I sat down, wrote the day and hour, the circumstances under which I awoke, together with my feelings and impressions. Several months after I received the sad news, that my beloved husband had expired the very night and hour he had so decidedly manifested himself to me in Paris. This was but a confirmation of what I knew. Twenty-six years have elapsed since that heartrending event, but I recollect it as vividly as if it had occurred last night. I shall never forget it."

Among the papers Madame Belzoni gave me is a prospectus, in French, dated 1829, with this heading: "*Dedicated by special permission to His Royal Highness the Duke of Clarence, Lord Grand Admiral, etc., etc., afterward William the Fourth.*" Its object was to announce a series of lithographs from unpublished original drawings of the great Egyptian tomb discovered by Belzoni in 1818. This conclusively shows that Belzoni's widow succeeded in making her situation known to his royal highness, before he became king of England in 1830. We further realize that even England's king knew, that one of his most deserving subjects, and that subject a lady, was without means in a strange country. Should not this most inexcusable of neglects (if neglect it can be called) take from him the surname, "*The Good King?*"

We have among these documents some curious and interesting papers, letters, and drawings, that would be foreign to obelisks and Freemasonry. There are also many of the mystery chambers in the Seti and Rameses Masonic temple we do not give in this epitome.

CHAPTER VII.

"Freemasonry has been of old, and will forever remain, the first requirement of a Freemason to possess a pair of clearly-seeing eyes."—RAGOTZSKY.

FROM a historic standpoint Freemasonry seems the growth of the world's elite in physical, intellectual, and moral science and progress, to which all times, tribes, nations, and races have furnished their quota, as may be realized by the following catalogue of the Masonic Alma Mater.

ANTEDILUVIAN ALUMNI.

ABEL * (Gen. 4, 2), 4001 B.C. *Abelites* are mentioned by St. Augustine as a sect in Africa. They reappeared as a secret or Masonic society in Germany, A.D. 1746, and were quite popular.

SETH (Gen. 4, 25), 3874 B.C., is held in high esteem, and considered by Masons as the earliest champion of esoteric Masonry.

JABAL (Gen. 4, 20), according to R. Macoy, was the first operative Mason.

TUBAL CAIN (Gen. 4, 22), 3454 B.C., "*instructor of every artificer in brass and iron,*" has ever been regarded as a primitive patron of Freemasonry. Naamah, in Hebrew, means "*the pleasant.*" The Masonic brethren regard her as the inventress of the spinning of wool and the weaving of cloth.

---

* We do not claim that secret or Masonic societies existed in the days of Abel, but that a sect and a Masonic brotherhood perpetuated his name by calling themselves *Abelites;* also that the Assyrian god Belus, Bel, or Baal, the Cretan Abelios, Celtic Bel, or Abellio, Greek and Roman Apollo, or Apello, were but modified names of the Hebrew HEBEL, from which our Abel was derived.

ENOCH (Gen. 5, 24) "walked with God, and was not; for God took him," 3017 B.C. This patriarch has been a mysterious personage in history and Masonry; the books attributed to him have been much discussed.

NOAH (Gen. 5, 29), 2348 B.C. Noachidæ and Noachites are considered high names by the members of the Mystic Tie.

POSTDILUVIAN ALUMNI.

JAPHET (Gen. 10, 1) is a Masonic personage, especially with the order of Ishmael. The European races regard him as their progenitor.

NIMROD (Gen. 10, 9), 2247 B.C., " the mighty hunter, the beginning of whose kingdom was Babel, Erech, Accad, and Calneh," has not been perpetuated by the Masonic Brothers; yet he must have been a patron of architecture in building those magnificent cities.

ASSHUR (Gen. 10, 11), 2247 B.C., who " builded Nineveh, the city of Rehoboth and Calah," is not mentioned in the Masonic annals. Neither is

CANAAN (Gen. 10, 15), 2247 B.C., after whom Canaan and the Canaanites were named ; nor is his son,

SIDON (Gen. 10, 15), who probably founded the great commercial emporium, Sidon; or was it named after him ? Such Grand Masters should be remembered.

PELEG (Gen. 10, 25), 2247 B.C., has been regarded by some archeologists and Masons as the architect of the Tower of Babel. He was, perhaps, the founder of the city of *Phaleg*, or Peleg, on the Euphrates, and progenitor of the Cyclopean builders, called *Pelasgi*. He is honorably mentioned by the Masonic craft. As Peleg means *division* in Hebrew, it is claimed that in his day the dispersion of the families and tribes commenced in the valley of the Euphrates.

MIZRAIM (Gen. 10, 6), 2247 * B.C., Herodotus' *Menes*, figures in Masonic records. The land of the lower Nile was settled by this patriarch and called after him, *Mazar* in hieroglyphs; but subsequently the Greeks named it Αιγυπτος (Egypt), after a son of Belus, king of Phenicia. The Arabs have ever called it *Mizr*, and call it so now.

ABRAHAM (Gen. 11, 27), 1921 B.C., whom European and American Freemasonry only name in connection with Melchizedek, has ever been revered by the ancient oriental order of Ishmael. It seems to us Abraham must have belonged to some institution like modern Freemasonry, otherwise he would not have been so readily and kindly received by the king of Egypt, the king of Salem, and other magnates of Canaan. According to eminent Egyptologists the Canaanites had previously conquered northeastern Egypt and established the three Dynasties of shepherd kings, who reigned from 2398 to 1703, B.C.

MELCHIZEDEK (Gen. 14, 18), "king of Salem and priest of the most high God," is mentioned with reverence by the Masonic Fraternity.

ISHMAEL. There is quite a powerful order under the name of Hagar's son. It has ramifications in most countries of the East and West, and includes Christians, Mahometans, Brahmans, Jews, and Parsees. Two of its chiefs reside in the orient, and one in the occident.

JOB. This Arabian prince and patriarch is cited as an exemplar to higher grades of the order of Ishmael. His book throws much light on the social and intellectual status of his period. It has induced much speculation.

---

* Although we consider Seyffarth's chronology, based on astronomical calculations, most correct, we follow Usher's, because it is yet in general use. According to Seyffarth, Mizraim emigrated from Shinar to Egypt 2783 B.C., and became its first king. This was the date of the confusion of language and the dispersion of Noah's progeny, which spread to Assyria, Canaan, Egypt, Phenicia, etc.

JOSEPH also is much revered by the widespread order of
Ishmael. Eminent Egyptologists claim that Joseph
was made regent of Egypt by Pharaoh Osirtasen I.,
the original Sesostris, 2186 B.C. They think the name
Zaphnath paaneah, translated from hieroglyphs, sig-
nifies grand vizier, and is the same as Hebrew *Iosaph*.
Even now the Afghan mountaineers have a tribe,
called *Eusofzie*, who are considered as descendants
of Joseph, through one of the "Ten Lost Tribes"
that settled in Afghanistan under Nebuchadnezzar.
Sir William Jones and other philologists say the
Afghan or Pushtoo language has much analogy with
Hebrew and Chaldaic. The late Hyneman believed
Freemasonry originated with Joseph.

EGYPTIAN MYSTERIES.*

These mysteries were very secret, very severe in their
trials, and connected with the esoteric worship of the deities of Egypt. The principal seat of the mysteries was at
Memphis, the ancient capital of Lower Egypt. They were
of two kinds—the greater and the less. The former were
devoted to Osiris and Serapis, the latter to Isis. The mysteries of Osiris were celebrated at the autumnal equinox,
those of Serapis at the summer solstice, and those of Isis at
the vernal equinox. The character of the candidate was
rigidly inquired into, and if report was unfavorable, exclu-
sion was certain. He was prepared for initiation by a period of fasting, and by peculiar ceremonies, calculated to
inspire him with religious awe.

The Isiac mysteries would seem to be the first degree
among the Egyptians. The second degree consisted of the
Mysteries of Serapis. Of their nature we know scarcely
anything. In the Mysteries of Osiris, which completed the

---

* We cull from Mackenzie's "*Royal Masonic Cyclopedia*," pp. 188 and 189.

series of Egyptian esoteric teaching, the lesson of death and resurrection of Osiris was symbolically conveyed; the legend of the murder and restoration of Osiris was displayed to the affiliate in a scenic manner. The legend itself was that Osiris, a wise king of Egypt, left the care of the kingdom to Queen Isis, and set forth to communicate the secrets of civilization to other nations. Isis here represents Egypt, and Osiris the sun. During his absence his brother, Typhon, conspired against his throne, and on the return of Osiris, Typhon, in the month of November, invited him to a banquet, where he produced a chest (ark, pastos, or coffin) inlaid with gold, promising to give it to any person, then present, whose body it would fit. Osiris laid himself down in the chest, when the lid was immediately closed, and he was cast into the Nile. The body of Osiris was tossed about by the waves, and finally cast on shore at Byblos, in Phenicia, at the foot of a tamarisk tree. Isis, in lamentation, traversed the whole world in search of the body, which had been mutilated, but recovered it at last, and brought it in triumph to Egypt, where it was committed to the tomb. She is variously represented as the mother, wife, and sister, of Osiris, the judge and father of the world of spirits.

SETI I., or Osymandias, and his son, RAMESES II., or Sesostris. Their rock-excavated Masonic Temple, beautifully adorned, was discovered by Belzoni, A.D. 1818. We think all in this magnificent structure indicates, that there was the origin of modern Freemasonry; for the attitudes, groups, rites, ceremonies, symbols, and signs, have a striking similarity both with Medieval and Modern Freemasonry. We are sorry we could not give all of the mystery chambers in this epitome.

CHAPTER VIII.

MOSES AND THE ISRAELITES.

MOSES has an exoteric and esoteric significance with Freemasons, who mention and invoke him in their Rites and high degrees. They accept Usher's chronology, 1451, B.C., as the date of his death. Egyptologists differ widely on this point: Prof. Seyffarth claims that Thothmes III., originator of the obelisk now on its way to New York, was the Pharaoh before whom Moses pleaded the deliverance of the Israelites, about 1866 B.C. This German savant bases this date on planetary configurations, as may be realized by his "Summary of Recent Discoveries," etc., p. 124, and his erudite essay, published in the Philadelphia *Sunday-School Times*, May 1, 1880.

Bunsen, Brugsch, Lepsius, Rosellini, Wilkinson, de Rougé, Chabas, Maspéro, Pierret, Mariette, etc., disagree with Seyffarth as to Thothmes and the date 1866; for most of them say Moses was born during the long joint reign of Seti I. and Rameses II., and that the Exodus occurred under Seti II. or Menephtah, son and successor of Rameses II.

Brugsch tells us in his "*Histoire d'Egypte*," p. 157: "As Rameses II. reigned 66 years, the reign of his successor, under whom the Exodus occurred, embraced 20 years; and, as Moses was 80 years old at the time of the Exodus, the children of Israel left Egypt in one of the last six years of Menephtah's reign, namely, between 1327 and 1321 B.C. If we admit that this Pharaoh perished in the sea, as reported

THE OBELISK AND FREEMASONRY. 73

in the Scriptures, Moses was born 80 years before 1321, or 1401 B.C., the sixth year of Rameses' reign."

We read in De Rougé's "*Notice des Monuments Egyptiens du Musée du Louvre,*" p. 22: "The circumstances of Hebrew history can therefore only apply to the epoch when the family of Rameses was on the throne. Moses, obliged to flee from the anger of the king after the murder of an Egyptian, suffered a long exile, because Rameses II. reigned more than 67 years. Soon after his return, Moses commenced the struggle which ended in the Exodus. This event, therefore, happened under the son of Rameses II., or, latest, during the period of troubles that followed his reign."

We read in Chabas' "*Recherches pour servir à l'Histoire de la XIX. Dynastie,*" p. 148: "The reign of Rameses II. alone agrees with the indispensable conditions, etc. . . . . We could not assign Moses to any other period, unless we entirely disregarded the Biblic account."

Maspéro, in his recent book "*Histoire Ancienne des Peuples de l'Orient,*" p. 286, tells us: "It is certain that Moses took the Israelites out of Egypt, gave them laws, and led them to the frontiers of Canaan, about the reign of Rameses III.," who, according to Gliddon, is the *Rameses, Sesostris,* and *Osymandias* of the Greeks, and reigned about 1565 B.C.

In Mariette Bey's "Aperçu de l'Histoire d'Egypte," p. 121, we read this significant passage: "*Que Moïse vécut sous Ramses II., et que Menephtah fut le Pharon de l'Exode est dorénavant un fait acquis a la science.*"*

Now, let us see how these learned Egyptologists differ as

---

* "That Moses lived under Rameses II., and that Menephtah was the Pharaoh of the Exodus, is henceforth a fact acquired to science." We need hardly state that Menephtah was the son of Rameses II., and was named Seti II., after his grandfather, Seti I., who was the Osymandias of the Greeks, and that Rameses II., surnamed the Great, was the Sesostris of the Greeks; so that, according to these accounts, Moses was born and lived under the greatest Eyyptian kings.

to the beginning of Rameses' reign, and consequently about the time when Moses lived:

Rosellini	1729 B.C.
Champollion	1723 "
Seyffarth	1693 "
Usher	1577 "
Gliddon	1565 "
Brugsch Bey	1407 "
Mariette Bey	1405 "
Lepsius	1388 "
Bunsen	1352 "
Wilkinson ("Ancient Egyptians," B.I., pp. 52–55*)	1355 "
Poole	1283 "

As these dates differ four hundred and forty-six years, it might be advisable to abandon Egyptian chronology till Pharaoh Psammetichus I., 666 B.C., about whose reign chronologists agree. If Moses lived under Thothmes III., 1866 B.C., there is a difference of 583 years between Seyffarth and Poole.

Moses needs no date, no chronology. The conception, primitiveness, and style of his writings are intrinsic evidence of remote traditional antiquity, which only required a master mind to portray and pen it; and that master mind appeared, when conditions and circumstances were favorable, neither before nor after. What should we know about those comparatively civilized personages, families, tribes, and nations of south-western Asia and north-eastern Africa, who for ages intermingled in the valleys of the Euphrates, Tigris, Jordan, and Nile, without the *Pentateuch?* What should we know concerning that almost sealed peninsula,

---

* Whoever will take the trouble to read the cogent dissertation on Moses and the Exodus, by Wilkinson and Lord Prudhoe, will find the strongest plea for placing the birth of Moses under the joint reign of Seti I. and Rameses II., and the Exodus under Seti II., or Menephtah, son and successor of Rameses II.

called *Arabia*, where, for mutual protection, the Nomade Bedouins have cherished a kind of Freemasonry since Ishmael, whom they now invoke as they did four thousand years ago?

As we already alluded to the widely diffused order of Ishmael, we need say no more.

Moses may even do without a *hieroglyphic cartouche*. However, one may yet be found and deciphered; for Egyptology is but of yesterday. Already linguists, who searched the Coptic or ancient Egyptian language, tell us *Mo* means *water*, and *ushe*, *saved*, which correspond to the statement of Josephus (Ant., B. II., c. 9, § 5), where we read: "The Egyptians call water '*Mo*,' and such as are saved from it '*uses;*' so that by putting these two words together they imposed the name (Moses) upon him."

Brugsch says, in his "*Histoire d'Egypte*" (pp. 157 and 173), *Mes* or *Messon* means a child born to one of the princes of Ethiopia under Rameses II.

We read in Arabic traditions that *Mo* in Egyptian means *water* and *se* signifies tree. Hence, the Arabs derive Moses from those two words, because he was found in the water among trees. The Arabs have to this day called Sinai *Jebel Musa* (Mount Moses).

It has lately been claimed that the "Lost Tribes" settled in the mountains of Afghanistan. Among them is one called *Moosa*. Linguists think this tribe assumed the name of the great Jewish leader, and bore it ever since. Thus does language corroborate the *Mosaic* career.

We might adduce Diodorus Siculus, Philo, Clemens of Alexandria, Eusebius, and more of Josephus, but we shall only add a passage from Strabo,* who lived from about 60 B.C. to 24 A.D.: "An Egyptian priest named Moses, who possessed a portion of the country of Lower Egypt . . . . being dissatisfied with the established institutions there, left it and came to Judea with a large body of people who wor-

---

* Strabo: B. XVI., c. II., § 35.

shiped the Divinity. He declared and taught, that the Egyptians and Africans entertained erroneous sentiments, in representing the Divinity under the likeness of wild beasts and cattle of the field; that the Greeks also were in error in making images of their gods after the human form, for God may be the one thing which encompasses us all, land and sea, which we call heaven, or the universe, or the Nature of things.

Who, then, of any understanding, would venture to form an image of this Deity, resembling anything with which we are conversant? On the contrary, we ought not to carve any images, but to set apart some sacred ground and a shrine, worthy of the Deity, and to worship Him without any similitude.

He taught, that those, who made fortunate dreams were to be permitted to sleep in the temple, where they might dream both for themselves and others; that those who practised temperance and justice, and none else, might expect good, or some gift or sign from the god from time to time.

By such doctrine Moses persuaded a large multitude of right-minded persons to accompany him to the place where Jerusalem now stands, etc. . . . . Instead of arms, he taught that their defence was in their sacred things and the Divinity, for whom he was desirous to find a settled place, promising to the people to deliver such a kind of worship and religion as should not burden those who adopted it with great expense, nor molest them with divine possessions, nor other absurd practices.

Moses thus obtained their good opinion, and established no ordinary kind of government. All the nations around willingly united themselves with him, allured by his discourses and promises."

CHAPTER IX.

HINDU MYSTERIES.

THE ancient Hindus practised initiatory rites and ceremonies in rock-excavated subterranean temples, as did the Egyptians in the Temple of Seti I. and Rameses II, discovered by Belzoni, 1818. James Fergusson's "*History of Indian Architecture*," pp. 437–447, describes them; and in his "*Rock-cut Temples*," he gives a beautiful illustration (Plate No. 8) of the Salsette rock-cut Temple. Mr. Erskine has an exhaustive description of the subterranean Temple of Elephanta in the Asiatic Journal. This renowned temple is in the Isle of Gharipour in the Gulf of Bombay. It is 135 feet square, 18 feet high, supported by four massive pillars; its walls are covered with sculptures and decorations. The western entrance to, and exit from were only accessible to the initiated. Chambers for various purposes led out of that temple. It has been regarded as one of the most ancient structures on the globe, and in it the Mysteries of India were celebrated, just as some of the Egyptian were solemnized in the Temple of Seti and Rameses. The German Indologist, Lassen, in his great work, "*Indische Alterthumskunde*," pp. 522–524, speaks of those colossal rock-excavated temples, whose construction he ascribes to the first century of our era, claiming they had no connection with those of Egypt. Should the German savant chance to hear of, or see the discoveries of Belzoni, Commander Gorringe, and Grand Master Zola, he might probably change his hastily conceived and expressed opinions; for the learned author of "*The Royal Masonic Cyclopedia*," Mackenzie, prior to these recent discoveries, considered the Hindu subterranean temples nearly cotemporaneous with those of Egypt, and if there was any difference in age, it would be in favor of Egypt, so that he is inclined to think, that the Hindus borrowed from Egypt. As this eminent student of Freemasonry has such a graphic description of the Hindu Mysteries, p. 315, we quote:

"The ceremony of the admission of a Brahman took place in a spacious cavern, such as that of Elephanta or Salsette. The whole course comprehended four degrees, the probationer commencing at the early age of eight. In this degree—analogous to the modern French rite of the adoption of a male child *—the actual ceremony consisted only of an investiture in a linen garment, and the girding on of the sacred zennaar, or cord of three strands, nine times twisted. Sacrifices, lustrations, and certain dedicatory words accompanied this form, and the candidate was next committed to the care of a Brahman, who prepared him by fasts and other austerities for the second degree. The second degree was an exaggeration of the first, and, as in the fellow-craft degree, the aspirant was made to turn his attention to the sciences, especially that of astronomy, which in those days was identical with astrology. Duly instructed in these main essentials, the disciple was led into a gloomy cavern, in which the aparrheta were to be displayed to him. Here a striking similarity to the Masonic system may be found: the three chief officers, or hierophants, representing Brahma, Vishnu, and Siva, are seated in the east, west, and south, attended by their respective subordinates.† After an invocation to the sun, an oath was demanded of the aspirant to the

---

* Here modern Freemasonry admits a simile and precedent from ancient India. Yet some of the learned brothers now claim, that their craft dates but to yesterday, namely, 1717 A.D. ; while others are willing to see its origin in the Dark Ages and Crusades, as though time and respectable ancestry were of little or no account.

† Another admission of analogy between ancient eastern and modern western Masonry. Yet, according to some of our sages, their craft dates but to 1717 A.D., or to the Crusades ! ! !

effect of implicit obedience to superiors, purity of body, and inviolable secrecy. Water was then sprinkled over him;* he was deprived of his sandals or shoes, and was made to circumambulate the cavern thrice, with the sun. Suitable addresses were then made to him, after which he was conducted through seven ranges of caverns in utter darkness, and the lamentations of Mahadeva, or the Great Goddess, for the loss of Siva, similar to the wailings of Isis for Osiris, † were imitated. After a number of impressive ceremonies, the initiate was suddenly admitted into an apartment of dazzling light, redolent with perfume and radiant with all the gorgeous beauty of the Indian clime, alike in flowers, perfumes, and gems. This represented the Hindu Paradise and the acme of all earthly bliss. This was supposed to constitute the regeneration of the candidate, and he was now invested with the white robe and the tiara; a peculiar cross was marked on his forehead, and the tau cross‡ on his breast, upon which he was instructed in the peculiar signs, tokens, and lectures of the order. He was presented with the sacred girdle, the magical black stone, the talismanic jewel for his breast, and the serpent-stone, which guaranteed him from the effects of poison. Finally, he was given the sacred word AUM, significative of the creative, preservative, and destructive powers of the Trimurti—Brahma, Vishnu, and Siva. With this the second degree concluded. The third degree comprehended a total isolation in the forests, when contemplation was enjoined as a duty, and sacrifice, together with abstinence, became a daily rite. In the fourth degree the Brahman was, by peculiar ceremonies, conjoined to the divinity and assured of future acceptance among the blessed."

Advanced Masons will realize, while perusing this, how

---

* Baptism ?

† Here the erudite Lassen might see some connection between Indian and Egyptian rites and ceremonies.

‡ Seven different crosses used in modern Freemasonry; yet nothing dates back of 1717 and beyond the Crusades !

much has reached their craft from the rock-excavated temples of India, especially from the second Brahmanic degree, which, surely, antedated both the Dark Ages and Crusades.

MAGI. We cannot omit the ancient Oriental order, styled *Magi*, who roamed for ages over the Asiatic plains, extending from the Jordan to the Indus, and from the Indian Ocean to the Caspian Sea, gazing at the stars, studying their course, and deducing therefrom what has been called *astrology*. They have also been known as the Wise Men of the East. They were a secret order, attributed to Zoroaster, prophet of the Medes and Persians, whom some ancient archeologists placed 6000 and others 700 B.C. The Parsees, now in India, are the only survivors of that worthy race. They have preserved Zoroaster's precepts in the Zend Avesta, which they consider as Christians do the Bible. They are to Asia what the Quakers are to Europe and America—sober, honest, and industrious citizens.

CHAPTER X.

ELEUSINIAN MYSTERIES.

THOSE rites and ceremonies in honor of the Greek *Demeter*, called *Ceres* by the Romans, have ever excited the world's curiosity and sharpened the acumen of critics. The eminent Orientalist, Lenormant, in a learned article published by that searching periodical *The Contemporary Review*, May, 1880, traces the *Eleusinia* to the Pelasgi of Arcadia, to the Thrakians, of Thrakia, and to *Eumolpus*, son of Poseidon and Chione, daughter of Boreas. We can assent to the Pelasgi, to the Thrakes, and to Eumolpos, but Poseidon (Neptune), Chione, and Boreas seem rather mythic. Greek and Roman authors, from Homer to Tacitus and Plutarch, have written about that ancient institution. Some ascribe it to Inachus, founder of Argos, 1800 B.C.; others to Erectheus, king of Athens; but Strabo tells us it florished under Cecrops, founder of Athens, 1556 B.C. As we only need, for our purpose, what transpired at the initiations, we shall glean and epitomize some of the principal details.

It is conceded that Eumolpos founded the Eleusinian Mysteries about 1356 B.C., that he became the first hierophant, and that this office was hereditary in his family, styled *Eumolpidæ*, for twelve centuries. The officiating personages consisted of

1. A male and a female hierophant, who directed the initiations.
2. A male and a female torch-bearer.
3. A male herald.

4. A male and a female altar attendant; and numerous minor officials.

There were *Lesser* and *Greater* Mysteries. The Lesser were celebrated at Agra every year, and the Greater at Eleusis every five years. Lenormant thinks little is known concerning the initiations; yet the following details have been gathered from various sources: Porphyry says the hierophant represented Plato's *Demiurgus,* or Creator of the world; the torch-bearer, the Sun; the altar-man, the Moon; the herald, Hermes, or Mercury; and the other officials, minor stars.

Men, women, and children were admitted; only criminals and outlaws were excluded. The examination of candidates was rigorous. The ancient Greeks thought the innocence of children could conciliate the gods with the initiated adults. To be initiated into the Lesser Mysteries, candidates had to keep themselves pure, chaste, and unpolluted for nine days, after which they came, offered sacrifices and prayers, wearing garlands of flowers. A year after this ceremony they sacrificed a sow to Demeter, or Ceres, and were admitted as candidates for the Greater Mysteries.

Crowned with myrtle and enveloped in robes, the novices passed into the *mystic temple* during the night. As they entered this vast building they washed their hands in *holy water,* * when they were told that they should come with a pure and undefiled mind, without which cleanliness of the body would not be acceptable. Next the holy mysteries were read to them from a large book,† called *Petroma,* because composed of two stones, fitly cemented together. The priest, styled hierophant, asked them some questions, which they readily answered; hymns were sung in honor of Ceres, while they proceeded.; soon the thunder rolled, lightning flashed, strange and fearful objects appeared, and the place seemed to shake and be on fire; hideous spectres glided

---

* Thence, probably, the *holy water* of the Romanists.
† Freemasons ever had a " *Book,*" and have one now.

through the building, moaning and sighing; frightful noises and howlings were heard. Mysterious apparitions, representing the messengers of the infernal deities, Anguish, Madness, Famine, Disease, and Death, flew around. As the trembling crowd of novices advanced amid this fearful spectacle, representing the torments of this life and those of *Tartarus*, they heard the solemn voice of the hierophant explaining them, and exhibiting his symbols of supreme deity, which but added to the horrors of the scene, when suddenly a serene light and objects of bliss appeared, and opened an *Elysium* to the initiated Eleusinian phalanx, who had, in a short time and space, experienced the miseries of Earth, the tortures of Tartarus, and the happiness of Elysium.

This initiation was styled *autopsy*, a term known to advanced Masons. When these ceremonies were ended, the officiating priest uttered the word *Konx*, which meant all was over, and those present could retire. The secrets were so sacred that, if any one disclosed them, it was supposed that he called divine wrath on himself; and it was unsafe to live in the same house with a wretch, that was publicly put to an ignominious death.

Every good Greek citizen was expected to become a member of this socio-religious institution; and the gravest charge against Socrates was that he had never joined it. Herodotus informs us (B. 9, 65), that the Persians burned the Temple of Eleusis, when they invaded Attica; but it was rebuilt, during the administration of Pericles, by *Ictinus*, architect of the Parthenon. During the sway of Demetrius Phalereus, the architect Philo added the portico of the twelve magnificent Doric columns. Strabo says the *mystic cell* of that splendid edifice could accommodate as many persons as the theatre. Then and there Greece had thousands of operatives and mechanics, directed by the *Dionysian architects*, whom we shall soon have occasion to mention.

Lodges and orders of our day may realize how much of the Eleusinian Mysteries is now retained in Masonic initiations.

The Goths under Alaric destroyed this splendid structure A.D. 396. The colossal statue of Ceres in the vestibule of the public library at Cambridge was brought from Eleusis (now Lepsina), by E. D. Clarke and Mr. Cripps, 1801. This beautiful relic of Greek art was the work of the renowned Phidias.

Thus, the mysteries of the Greco-Latin goddess of husbandry had lasted about eighteen centuries, when **Theodosins,** urged by some Fathers of the Church, abolished them, under the plea that they were immoral. As they had ever been celebrated publicly under the supervision of the State, we must refuse credence to this imputation. This early **interference** of the Fathers of the Church was a shadow of the coming papacy and subsequent Inquisition against free-thinkers and liberal associations. The imperial edict became later a precedent and plea for papal bulls and Inquisitorial tribunals.

Archeologists say these mysteries, rites, and festivals of Ceres were derived from similar ceremonies, performed in honor of Isis in Egypt. This seems probable, when we consider, that Cecrops led a colony from Egypt to Greece, founded Athens, and became its first king.

We devoted so much space to this earliest and most lasting European secret association, that has any analogy to medieval or modern operative and theoretic Masonry, because we thought it had rites, ideas, emblems and symbols, which resembled those of Egypt and India; especially the ordeal of horrors, nearly identical with those of Elephanta, now in vogue in oriental and in some western orders. The Eleusinian order had its male grand master, wardens, and minor officials. True, it admitted women and children, thus completing the social fabric; but it excluded criminals and outlaws. It had its grades and initiations, with social, moral, and religious bearings, and strictly enjoined secrets; so that every order or association, formed in Europe or America, either for social, moral, or religious purposes, or mutual protection, must point to Greece for a prototype. This gains

THE OBELISK AND FREEMASONRY. 85

yet more force, when we trace the Eleusinia to the imposing order, that initiated Pharaohs, princes, queens, hierophants, priests, and magnates in the magnificent secluded Masonic Temple, constructed by *Seti* I. (Osymandias) and his son, *Rameses* II. (Sesostris), which looks more like modern Freemasonry than anything history mentions, and of which every intelligent Mason must feel proud, when he inspects and studies Belzoni's atlas, especially Plate 19.

CURETES. Priests of Cybele, mother of the gods in Crete, were probably coëval with the establishment of the Eleusynian Mysteries. The initiation into this ancient order lasted 27 days, during which the candidate was confined in a cave, which reminds of the Egyptian and Hindoo subterranean Masonic Temples. It has been claimed, that Pythagoras belonged to this order.

CHAPTER XI.

DIONYSIAN MYSTERIES.*

"CELEBRATED throughout Hellas and Ionia, but chiefly at Athens, they were introduced from Egypt into Greece in honor of Dionysos or Bacchus. The legend of the murder of Dionysos was commemorated in their ceremonies. In the outset of these mysteries was shown the consecration of the mundane egg, of which all Eastern religions, from Japan, India, Burmah, and the Hellenic countries, make mention. Lustration by water having taken place, the candidate was crowned with a myrtle branch, introduced into the sacred vestibule, and clothed in the sacred habiliments. He was then delivered to the conductor, who proclaimed in a loud voice, '*Depart hence, all ye profane!*'† After exhortations to the candidate, enjoining fortitude and courage, he was led through dark caverns, termed by Stobœus a rude and fearful march through night and darkness. Here wild beasts howled, and artificially produced thunder and lightning prevailed, while monstrous apparitions were from time to time shown through the gloom. These scenes continued for three days and nights, after which the mystic death of Bacchus or Dionysos, displayed in the person of the candidate, began to be enacted. The candidate was now placed on the pastos, couch, or coffin, and closely confined in a chamber where, in solitude, he was left to all the horrors of the situation. Typhon, searching for Osiris—the legends being the same,

---

* Mackenzie's "*Royal Masonic Cyclopedia,*" p. 158.

† Virgil, B. VI. : "*Procul, procul, este profani!*" The same proclamation is made during the Eleusynian Mysteries by the herald.

—seeks for the ark, in which he is inclosed, and rends it into pieces by his mighty power, scattering the limbs upon the waters, upon which arise mournful lamentations on the decease of the god. Rhea or Isis then begins her search for the remains of Dionysos or Osiris, and indescribable howlings ensue, made by the priests and assistants at the ceremony, until, at a signal from the Hierophant, mourning is changed into rejoicing—the body is found, and the candidate released, amid shouts of, We have found it!—let us rejoice together! The candidate was next made to descend into Tartarus,* or the infernal regions, and behold the blessings and happiness of the good and punishment of the wicked. He was then, like the modern initiates of Freemasonry, given a new vestment of white, and received among the number of the Epopts. By this series of trials he was supposed to receive regeneration, and, of course, public consideration and rank were the due meed of every individual favored enough, or courageous enough, to undergo the ordeal."

No doubt, these Mysteries prepared the way for the

DIONYSIAN ARCHITECTS.†

At a very early period in the historic times of the world we find in existence a wandering *guild* of builders, consecrated to Dionysos or Bacchus. They made their appearance certainly not later than 1000 B.C., and appear to have enjoyed particular privileges and immunities. They also possessed secret means of recognition, and were bound together by special ties only known to themselves. The richer of this fraternity were bound to provide for their poorer brethren.‡ They were divided into communities, governed

---

* Perhaps the *deep, rock-excavated, dark well* in the Temple of Seti I. and Rameses II. was the prototype of the Dionysian Mysteries.

† Mackenzie's "*Royal Masonic Cyclopedia,*" p. 157.

‡ This Fraternity of architects and masons was no doubt one of the early orders, similar to medieval and modern Freemasonry; because founded on mutual protection and charity.

by a Master and Wardens, and called γυνοικιαι (connected houses). They held a grand festival annually, and were held in high esteem. Their ceremonials were regarded as sacred. It has been claimed that Solomon, at the instance of Hiram, King of Tyre, employed them at his temple and palaces. They were also employed at the construction of the Temple of Diana at Ephesus. They had means of intercommunication all over the then known world, and from them, doubtless, sprang the guilds of the Traveling Masons known in the Middle Ages.

To this ancient charitable institution, dating back three thousand years, our mutual labor associations may point with pride; for to these enterprising architects, employed by kings and hierophants, Parthenons, Mausoleums, and all of the Greek and Roman monuments owed their existence. Ephesus, Rhodes, Athens, Rome, Constantinople, etc., point to them as their beautifiers. In the Dionysian architects the modern Brothers cannot help seeing theoretic and operative prototypes.

SOLOMON is so well known by Freemasons, that we need not enlarge on his Masonic attributes. Those, who wish to know his career, may read his books and consult 2 Sam., v., 11; 1 K., v., vi., vii., viii., ix.; and 1 Chr., xiv., etc. Also Josephus, Eusebius, Clemens, and Alexander Polyhistor will enlighten them on the career of that strange mixture of wisdom and folly. His temple has ever been the theme of operative and theoretic Masons. Its pillars *Jachin* and *Boaz* have been Masonic household words among the Brethren of the Magic Tie. Not only Jews and Christians, but Arabs have remembered Solomon. Freemasons have pointed to him as the first Masonic Grand Master. We suppose, after the discoveries of Belzoni and Commander Gorringe, they will look beyond Solomon's temple to Rameses' rock-cut Temple, recognize Rameses II. (Sesostris) as the first

Masonic Grand Master, and adopt his sun and serpent apron.

HIRAM has ever been indissolubly connected with Solomon. We are told these two kings formed an intellectual bond between commercial Tyre and religious Jerusalem. Those, who desire to know more about Hiram, will find it in the same chapters of 1 Kings, which give the career of both. The great Jewish temple seems to have engaged the attention of Hiram and Solomon for about seven years. But King Hiram's name lives now in a famous monument near the site of Tyre. It is a sarcophagus of limestone, hewn out of a single block twelve feet long, eight wide, and six high, covered by a lid slightly pyramidal, and five feet in thickness, the whole resting on a massive pedestal about ten feet high. A tradition, received by all classes and sects of that country, calls it "*Kabr Hairan*" (Tomb of Hiram). The people of that region also connect Hiram's name with a fountain, over which a massive stone structure has been raised. It is not far from the ruins of Tyre. Thus has the name of Hiram, Solomon's friend, been perpetuated from the days of Tyre's grandeur.

HIRAM ABIF. While Kings Solomon and Hiram are considered theoretic Masons, Hiram Abif may be regarded as the operative Mason at the structure of the temple. It has been claimed, that the Dionysian architects arose in, and had their main association at, Tyre, and that Hiram Abif was of their craft. This distinguished Tyrian artisan is honorably mentioned in 1 K. vii. 13–46. Even now Freemasons have a tool named Hiram.

ADONIRAM, Solomon's treasurer and financier, was a very useful personage in the carrying out Solomon's architectural plans.

SACRED LODGE. We are told this lodge was held in the bowels of Mount Moriah, under the part, on which was erected the Sanctum Sanctorum of the temple. Solomon, King Hiram, and Hiram Abif presided over this ancient Masonic institution. Was it copied from Rameses' rock-excavated Temple in Egypt or from the temple of Elephanta, in India? We are told Oriental *Dervis* hold now their secret meetings in subterranean temples; so that the custom has continned four thousand years.

CHAPTER XII.

MYSTERIES OF THE DRUIDS.

THERE were three degrees: 1. Bards, or chanters. 2. Prophets, or spaiers. 3. Druids, or sanctified authorities, from whose judgment there was no appeal. In Albion, now England, there were provinces under an Arch-Druid, invested with supreme authority. Under him was a trinity of ministers, and twenty-five subordinates, deans, or deacons. The assembly of the Druids met annually for the judgment of causes and enactment of rules, and four other meetings took place, as near as possible to the equinoctial and solsticial periods * of the year. They had secret passwords, and adored *Hu*, the mighty Hu. Initiates were made under the canopy of heaven, the place of meeting was to be unpolluted with a metal tool, and those belonging to the order were invested with a chain. The colors were *white, blue,* and *green—light, truth,* and *hope*. A *pastos*, or coffin,† was required, and the progress of the initiates was gradual. After severe trials he was admitted to the privileges of Druidism. The following principles were instilled into the candidate at progressive stages: 1. That all worthy things descend from the Heaven of Heavens. 2. The soul, after death, goes into divers other bodies; the sublimer minds ascend to higher orbs than our earth, there to enjoy

---

* The Dionysian Mysteries were solemnized at the same periods in Greece; hence analogy between the Dionysian and Druidic Mysteries.

† We find the same custom in the Dionysian and Egyptian Mysteries. In Seti's temple, in two of the chambers, is a *pastos*, so that the Druids must have borrowed from the Greeks and Egyptians, or the Greeks and Egyptians from the Druids.

unbounded felicity. 3. Whatever is left with the dying, or is cast upon their funereal-pyres, is surely theirs in the other world. 4. Those who destroy themselves will go thither with their friends, and there abide with them. 5. None shall receive instruction without the limits of our sacred grove; there the oak and mistletoe favor devotion. 6. The education of children demands the greatest care; twenty years of assiduous teachings will scarce suffice. 7. The secrets of our sciences and arts must not be committed to writing; they must repose in the memory alone.* 8. Every soul is immortal, however long and variously it may transmigrate. 9. The mistletoe must never be cut but with a golden bill, and, if possible, only in the sixth moon; it is to be gathered with a holy reverence, and, when deposited in the white sagum, must be then conveyed, upon two white bulls, to the place where needed. 10. The powder of the mistletoe is salutary for women, making them fruitful. 11. The sacrifices are holy; none but the obedient shall attend them. 12. Man or woman may be sacrificed on extraordinary occasions. 13. Prisoners of war are to be slain at times, and upon the cromlechs; or they may be burned alive within the wickers, in honor of the immortal gods. 14. Future events may be foretold from the direction, in which the body falls, when seized by death, or as the same shall move when fallen, or as the blood may flow therefrom. 15. Strangers must have no commerce with our people, save from necessity, or for some good unto ourselves. 16. Children are to be brought up separate from their parents, until their fourteenth year; the foundation must be laid by their ghostly fathers. 17. When the world is destroyed it must

---

* This seems to have been, and is now, the custom of the Bedouin Arabs, who pride themselves on their oral traditions. Such a custom has ever more or less prevailed among the Oriental races. Initiations and secrecy were the order of the day, and when they did write they only wrote the consonants and omitted the vowels; or hieroglyphs; hence our Celtic ancestors brought that usage with them from the East at a very remote period.

be by fire or by water. 18. Money lent, and not repaid, will be restored in the next world. 19. Every one who comes sluggishly to the assembly of our states, and he who is the last of all in attendance, shall surely die! 20. The earth we inhabit is not a plain, but a globe; and so are the sun, moon, and stars likewise. 21. All light comes from the sun; that which by the moon is shed is but borrowed by him from her. 22. Our people were mighty in knowledge once. Upon the heights of Caer-Idris, also at Cerrig Brudyn, and at Myfyrion, they were used to meditate upon the heavenly bodies; and there did they contemplate all nature; the mysteries were there taught unto our youth; and, in the plains below, our wise men saw that the wisdom so gained was practised. 23. Temples are never to be raised with closed walls, and they are likewise to be open to the skies; they are to be upon the plains, or on some lofty height, that the heavenly spheres may be the better seen; and if upon the plains, then in the open air, and yet with trees encompassing. 24. No images of the gods have we, but emblems only; hence does the truncated oak symbolize both the firmness and the majesty of the god of gods. 25. Our Faids, also called *Vacerri*, are the ordinary priests; the *Eubages* are our augurs; the *Bardi*, also called *Vates*, are our poets and chroniclers; the *Vergobretus* does judge the law; and the *Saronidæ* instruct our youths, and also administer justice, under the guidance of the Arch-Druids and of the Vergobretus. Such is the order and creed of the Druids.

According to our reading of history, the *priesthoods* of Belus, or Baal, in Assyria, of Osiris, in Egypt, of Jehova, in Palestine, of Jupiter, in Greece and Rome, of Ahura Mazda, in Persia, of Brahma, in India, and of Teutates, in Britain, were *primitive secret societies*, who instructed and governed the primitive families and races. It little matters whether we call the members of those priesthoods *Belites, Pastophori, Levites, Curetes, Magi, Brahmins,* or *Druids;* they were connected by secret ties, and intercommunicated from the Indus to the Tiber, from the Nile to the Thames. Hence there ever has been, is, and ever will be Freemasonry on our planet. Masonry was ever more or less connected with priesthoods till about the thirteenth century of our era, when Masons declared themselves *Freimaurer* (Freemasons). Since about that period priesthoods have ever denounced and persecuted Freemasonry.

NUMA POMPILIUS, about 650 B.C., lawgiver of the Romans, founder of the College of the Pontifices (High Priests) of the Augurs, of the Flamens, and of the Vestals, and of the Temple of Janus, we consider as a worthy Mason of his epoch. His reconciling the Romans and Sabines shows he was a peacemaker, and his consulting Egeria in the grove indicates, that he was somewhat of a Druid, which he may have shared with the Celtic and Etrurian races then in Italy. All his institutions are of a Masonic type.

PYTHAGORAS, 550 B.C., the greatest Masonic figure of antiquity, joined the Curetes, and became, no doubt, an initiate of the Eleusinian Mysteries. After having studied under Greek philosophers, he went to Egypt, gazed at the pyramids, conversed with the hierophants, and was initiated into the Egyptian Mysteries in the rock-excavated Temple, constructed by Seti I. and Rameses II., known to the Greeks as *Osymandias* and *Sesostris*. On his way to India, the traveler stopped at Babylon, where he studied Chaldean Magic. In India he learned the doctrine of Metempsychosis from the Brahmins, who made him one of their initiates in the rock-excavated Temple of Elephanta.

Thus versed in Greek learning, and endowed with Egyptian, Chaldean, and Hindoo wisdom, Pythagoras was fully qualified to introduce a new educational curriculum. His degrees were: 1. *Mathematici;* 2. *Theoretici;* 3. *Electi.* Hence, mathematics, or the exact sciences, formed the basis of his pupils' education. Only after having been exact were they allowed to theorize; only after having been exact and theoretic were they permitted to be eclectic under the master's guidance. The city of Crotona, in Southern Italy, was chosen as the residence of this famous Brotherhood. Soon disciples flocked to it from all parts of the known world. Surrender of all property for the benefit of the order was one of the primary conditions. The fraternity was divided in two classes—*Exoterics* and *Esoterics*, whence these terms came into our modern language. Silence, secresy, and unconditional obedience were cardinal principles of the Pythagorean Order. The great teacher and reformer was universally respected for his integrity, but envied by knaves, who induced the mob of Crotona to burn his school. Thus, after an unexampled success of thirty years, was this famous Order of Sages destroyed, and its founder died poor, 506 B.C. On comparison, Freemasons of our day may realize, that they have much in common with the Fraternity of Crotona.

HERODOTUS, about 440 B.C., in his grand History of Antiquity, tells us much about Egypt, its laws, customs, and monuments. He also relates some of the conversations he had with priests; but he is very guarded not to tell us what he saw and experienced, while being initiated into the Egyptian Mysteries and into Masonry in the rock-excavated Temple of Seti I. and his son, Sesostris. As the great historian and traveler had probably been initiated into the Eleusinian Mysteries, the Egyptian initiations seemed no novelty. Since Belzoni, Commander Gorringe, Grand Master Zola and our Consul-General Farman, have discovered such decided marks of ancient Egyptian Masonry, we may infer possibilities.

PLATO, 400 B.C., it is claimed, visited the cradle of civilization, joined Egypt's secret order, and probably passed the grades, conferred in the rock-excavated Temple of Seti I. and Rameses II. (Sesostris). At that period Egypt must have been a strong magnetic centre, that could thus attract and initiate those ancient sages.

ESSENES. About the time of Jesus Christ arose an order of this name. This famous brotherhood was intermediary between the ancient and medieval Asiatic orders, being less priestly than its predecessors and embodying more science and practice in their daily lives. Jews, Assyrians, Egyptians, Arabs, Persians, and Greeks joined. On application, the candidate had to resign all his property for the common good of the Fraternity. The probation lasted three years, and comprised two degrees. On full admission the candidate received a spade, an apron, and a white robe. They lived in communities and did not marry. Secresy was one of their chief tenets. Eusebius and Philo tell us they could discover no difference between their mode of life and that of the first Christians. It is often claimed, that Jesus Christ belonged to the Essenean Brotherhood. Mostly scholars and men of distinction joined this order. The Essenes seem to have been very frugal and industrious men, and as such they did not attract large numbers. Some authors have ascribed to the members of that early order the writings of the New Testament. Josephus, in his "*Antiquities*," has much to say about those simple and frugal sages. There is some analogy between our Masonic orders and the Essenean Fraternity, which only lasted during the first centuries of our era. The Essenes lived principally in Palestine and Syria.

VITRUVIUS, 43 B.C., who has been considered as one of the famous brotherhood, styled the Dionysian Architects, perpetuated the institution, which extended over Greece and Rome, and pointed to Hiram Abif as its first Grand Master, 1000 B.C. Vitruvius served as a

THE OBELISK AND FREEMASONRY. 97

military engineer under Julius Cæsar in Africa, 43 B.C. He designed and cOnstructed a temple at Fanum. During the reign of Augustus he was inspector of engines. In his old age he wrote his great work on architecture, entitled, "*De Architecturâ*," which has ever been highly esteemed. It is divided into ten books, and is the only ancient treatise on architecture that reached us. Both operative and theoretic Masons may point to Vitruvius with pride.

AUGUSTUS CESAR, BARBARUS, and PONTIUS the Architect, 23 B.C. We rejoice to be able to record three distinguished Masons, belonging to the opening of the first century of our era. As previously mentioned, while Mr. Wynman Dixon, C.E., was examining the foundation of the pedestal of the standing twin obelisk at Alexandria, he found one of the brass crabs, used by the Romans as supports, and on the large claw of it was this inscription in Latin, which we translate here:

"In the eighth year of the reign of *Augustus Cesar* (23 B.C.), *Barbarus*, Prefect of Egypt, caused these obelisks to be erected by *Pontius*, the architect." Since the Masonic signs, emblems, and symbols, have been discovered around and under the pedestal of the American obelisk by Commander Gorringe, and endorsed by Grand Master Zola and Consul General Farman, the question arises: Who directly or indirectly ordered those obelisks to be raised? Had the emperor any direct or indirect share in the ordering, or was all left to the prefect? or did both emperor and prefect share in the ordering of the work, for which the State paid all expenses? Moreover, who knew about and ordered those emblematic and symbolic stones, that were to be deposited in a vault, constructed for the purpose? Surely, the architect Pontius did not do all that at his expense, which must have been considerable.

Some itemized bill had to be sent to the imperial treasurer. Hence we conclude, that the emperor, prefect, and architect, were all of the craft, and knew about it, which clearly proves that theoretic and operative Masonry of some kind existed in the very beginning of our era. No doubt, Pontius belonged to the ancient craft of the Dionysian architects, previously mentioned.

Augustus, who was ever deeply interested in literature, science, and art, would delight in knowing all about those venerable relics, that were to perpetuate his reign, and from sheer emulation the prefect would inform himself, so as to give a proper account to his master, the author of the "*Augustan Era.*" Therefore let us henceforth honor Augustus, Barbarus, and Pontius, as high Masons of their epoch. Thus did Masonry flourish on the Nile under Rameses the Great, hero of Kadish, about 1500 B.C. and under the great Augustus, hero of Actium, 31 B.C.

ST. LUKE, about A.D. 50, the Evangelist and author of "The Acts," has been regarded by some Masonic writers as a iatric (*healing*) Mason, which may be due to St. Paul's calling him "the beloved physician" (Col. iv. 14).

PLUTARCH, about A.D. 80, we are told, was an initiate of the Egyptian Mysteries. He mentions this inscription on the Temple of Isis: "I, Isis, am all that has been, that is, or shall be, and no mortal has ever unveiled me." *

APULEIUS,† A.D. 150, who had been initiated into all the Egyptian mysteries, speaks of those of Isis in the following way: "The priest—all the profane being removed to a distance—taking hold of me by the

---

* Madame Blavatski violated this solemn declaration of the Egyptian goddess by calling her great work "*Isis Unveiled*," published by James Bouton, 706 Broadway, New York.

† Metamorphosis, Book XI.

hand, brought me into the inner recesses of the sanctuary itself, clothed in a new linen garment. Perhaps, curious reader, you may be eager to know what was then said and done. I would tell you, were it lawful for me to tell you; you should know it, if it were lawful for you to hear; but both the ears that heard those things, and the tongue that told them, would reap the evil results of their rashness. Still, however, kept in suspense, as you probably are with religious longing, I will not torment you with long-protracted anxiety. Hear, therefore, but believe what is the truth. *I approached the confines of death*, and having trod on the threshold of Proserpine, I returned therefrom, being borne through all the elements. At midnight I saw the sun, shining with its brilliant light, and approached the presence of the gods beneath and the gods above, and stood near and worshiped them. Behold, I have related to you things of which, though heard by you, you must necessarily remain ignorant. It is most probable, that the mysteries of Isis alluded to her personification of Nature. In addressing Apuleius, she says: 'I am Nature, the parent of all things, the sovereign of the elements, the primary progeny of time.'"

Here we fully realize, that Egypt's Mysteries, and with them probably her Masonry in the rock-excavated Temple of Seti I. and Rameses II., florished as late as A.D. 150, when the Roman sage penned this passage; but soon societies of mutual aid and charity, Mysteries, and Masonic institutions will vanish before northern Vandals and Mahometan fanatics, and dark ages supervene.

THE GOTHO-GERMANIC AND SCANDINAVIAN MYSTERIES.

These mysteries are so wild and incoherent, that it would be difficult to give a concise idea of them. The *Edda and Nibelungen* contain them. The Celts, Cimbri, and Teutones were so mixed in Central, Western, and Northern Europe, that their dialects, customs, and manners assumed a similarity, from close and long intercourse. They all worshiped and celebrated their festivals in the open air, in groves and dismal forests. Odin or Woden was their Grand Master, and became their god. The *Rosicrucians* borrowed and embodied many of their ancestors' notions and customs, and mixed them with oriental ideas in the tenets of their order. The Sea-Kings and scalds of the Scandinavian races may be considered as their Grand Masters.

JAMBLICHUS, A.D. 306, who was thoroughly versed in the
Platonic ideas as found in Chaldean, Assyrian, and Eleusinian Mysteries, wrote a treatise, entitled "Egyptian Mysteries," and a "Life of Pythagoras," whose principles he taught. The works of this great writer, who florished during the reign of Constantine the Great (A.D. 306-337), contain many ideas, emblems, and symbols, cherished by medieval and modern Masons. The Rosicrucians warmly espoused the doctrines of Jamblichus, who felicitously blended the theories of the ancients in his writings. He chose Pythagoras as his model.

ANTHEMIUS (about A.D. 530), the architect of St. Sophia, at Constantinople, lived under the emperor Justinian, who employed him to design, plan, and construct St. Sophia. As he died A.D. 534, leaving the great edifice unfinished, Isidorus completed it, A.D. 537. No doubt, Anthemius was one of the noble Brotherhood, styled the "Dionysian Architects," who pointed to Hiram Abif as their first Grand Master, 1012 B.C., and subsequently spread from Phenicia and Asia

Minor over the Persian, Greek and Roman empires whose monuments and edifices they reared. From them, as will hereafter appear, the medieval Masonic associations and guilds obtained their ideas and constitutions of mutual protection and charity.

POPE BONIFACE IV., A.D. 614. We read that this liberal Pontiff granted to the Masonic guilds and corporations a Diploma, giving them the exclusive privilege to erect all religious buildings and monuments, and, by the same authority, made them *free* from all local, royal, or municipal statutes.*

This papal Diploma so elated masons, carpenters, and other crafts, that they associated, formed guilds, and traveled singly or in bands, in order to offer their services to bishops, abbots, priests, villages, towns and cities, where devotional buildings might be needed. Wherever they passed they obtained hospitality. In Germany the *Burschen* could be met singly or in bands, with knapsack on their back. Monasteries and convents vied in giving them hospitality. This state of things went on for several centuries. Meanwhile the crusades engrossed the attention of able-bodied mechanics, which tended to diminish the guilds. Another class of men, alchemists and Rosicrucians, sympathized with the guilds, and gradually all united, to which the church in vain took exception. Soon the intellect of the alchemists and Rosicrucians was felt among the guilds. Also the Crusaders formed secret associations, such as Templars, Hospitallers, or Knights of St. John, Teutonic Knights, all of whom had affiliations, at which the church grew alarmed and established the Inquisition; then she called on kings and princes to assist her in disbanding the guilds

---

* Was Boniface IV. a Mason ? If so, he was a noble prototype to Pius IX., who became a Mason in his youth, and betrayed Masonry in his old age.

and Crusaders she had previously encouraged. The Templars, who were the most powerful, were sacrificed, but without the decided effect that was expected. When Pope Clement V. and Philippe le Bel succeeded in murdering Grand Master Molay and sixty of his brethren, they thought they had given the death-blow to secret societies and Masonry; but they did not consider, that Masonry had such deep roots in the British Isles, that popes and kings could not destroy it, and, if they succeeded in destroying it on the Continent, it would spread again from the British Isles, as it ever has been, is, and will be spreading.

CHAPTER XIII.

"A Mason is a man, whose conduct should be squared by strict rectitude and justice to his fellow-creatures."—MACOY.

To realize the strength of Freemasonry in the British Isles any one has but to scan the following galaxy of eminent names from King Alfred the Great, A.D. 872, to His Royal Highness Albert Edward, Prince of Wales, K.G., as cited in Mackenzie's Cyclopædia.

A.D.
 287. St. Alban, Grand Master of Masonry in Britain.
 597. Austin the Monk, Master of Masonry in Britain.
 872. King Alfred the Great.*
 900. Ethred, King of Mercia.
 924. King Athelstan.
 926. Prince Edwin, brother of Athelstan.
 957. St. Dunstan, Archbishop of Canterbury.
1041. King Edward the Confessor, and Leofric, Earl of Coventry.
1066. Roger de Montgomery, Earl of Arundel and of Shrewsbury, and Gondulph, Bishop of Rochester.
1100. King Henry I.
1135. Gilbert de Clare, Marquis of Pembroke.

---

* We fully realize that King Alfred accomplished things, that required more than mere royalty, when he corresponded with Abel, Patriarch of Jerusalem, who informed Alfred of the wretched condition of the Christians in India, and when the English monarch sent the enterprising priest Sighelm, who started, fulfilled his mission, and returned safely; also when he sent Ohthere with a fleet to the Hyperborean tribes and countries, which also met with success. See our "*Origin, Progress, and Destiny of the English Language and Literature.*"

Only Alfred, being Grand Master of Masonry, accounts for the success of such distant enterprises at that early period.

1154. The Grand Master of the Templars, Bernard de Tremblay.
1176. Peter de Colechurch.
1212. William Almaine.
1216. Peter de Rupibus, Bishop of Winchester.
1234. Geoffrey Fitz Peter.
1272. Walter Giffard, Archbishop of York.
Gilbert de Clare, Earl of Gloucester.
Ralph, Lord of Mount Hermer.
1307. Walter Stapleton, Bishop of Exeter.
1327. King Edward III.
1350. John de Spoulee, Master of the Ghiblim.
1357. William de Wykeham, Bishop of Winchester.
1375. Robert de Barnham.
Henry Yevele, surnamed the King's Freemason.
Simon Langham, Abbot of Winchester.
1377. William de Wykeham (for a second time).
1399. Thomas Fitz-Allen, Earl of Surrey.
1413. Henry Chicheley, Archbishop of Canterbury.
1443. William Waynfleet, Bishop of Winchester.
1471. Richard Beauchamp, Bishop of Salisbury.
1485. King Henry VII., Grand Master of the Order of St. John.
1493. John Islip, Abbot of Westminster.
1502. Sir Reginald Bray.
1515. Cardinal Thomas Wolsey.
1539. Thomas Cromwell, Earl of Essex.
1540. John Touchett, Lord Audley.
1549. Edward Seymour, Duke of Somerset.
1551. John Poynet, Bishop of Winchester.
1561. Sir Thomas Sackville.
1567. Francis Russell, Earl of Bedford.
Sir Thomas Gresham.*

---

* London merchant, who built, at his own expense, the Royal Exchange, about 1566, and founded the college, called by his name, 1575. He was to London what Peter Fanueil was to Boston, Stephen Girard to Philadelphia, and what Peter Cooper, Astor, and Lenox have been to New York.

1579. Charles Howard, Earl of Effingham.
1588. George Hastings, Earl of Huntingdon.
1603. King James I.
1607. Inigo Jones, the architect.
1618. William Herbert, Earl of Pembroke.
1625. King Charles I.
1630. Henry Danvers, Earl of Danby.
1633. Thomas Howard, Earl of Arundel.
1635. Francis Russell, Earl of Bedford.
1636. Inigo Jones (a second time).
1660. King Charles II.
Henry Jermyn, Earl of St. Albans.
1666. Thomas Savage, Earl Rivers.
1674. George Villars, Duke of Buckingham.
1679. Henry Bennet, Earl of Arlington.
1685. Sir Christopher Wren, architect of St. Paul's Cathedral.
1695. Charles Lenox, Duke of Richmond.
1698. Sir Christopher Wren (a second time).
1717. Anthony Sayer, Esquire.
1718. George Payne, Esquire.
1719. J. T. Desaguliers, LL.D., F.R.S., savant and naturalist.
1720. George Payne, Esquire (a second time).
1721. John, Duke of Montagu.
1722. Philip, Duke of Wharton.
1723. Francis Scott, Earl of Dalkeith.
1724. Charles Lenox, Duke of Richmond.
1725. James Hamilton, Lord Paisley.
1726. William O'Brien, Earl of Inchiquin.
1727. Henry Hare, Lord Coleraine.
1728. James King, Lord Kingston.
1729-30. Thomas Howard, Duke of Norfolk.
1731. T. Coke, Lord Lovel, afterward Earl of Leicester.
1732. Anthoni Brown, Viscount Montacute.
1733. James Lyon, Earl of Strathmore.
1734. John Lindsay, Earl of Crawfurd.

1735. Thomas Thynne, Viscount Weymouth.
1736. John Campbell, Earl of Loudoun.
1737. Edward Bligh, Earl of Darnley.
1738. H. Brydges, Marquis of Carnarvon.
1739. Robert, Lord Raymond.
1740. John Keith, Earl of Kintore.
1741. James Douglas, Earl of Morton.
1742-3. John, Lord Dudley and Ward.
1744. Thomas Lyon, Earl of Strathmore and Kinghorn.
1745-6. James, Lord Cranstoun.
1747-51. William, Lord Byron.
1752-3. John Proby, Lord Carysfort.
1754-6. James Brydges, Marquis of Carnarvon.
1757-61. Sholto Douglas, Lord Aberdour.
1762-3. Washington Shirley, Earl Ferrers.
1764-6. Cadwallader, Lord Blayney.
1767-71. Henry Somerset, Duke of Beaufort.
1772-6. Robert Edward, Lord Petre.
1777-81. George Montagu, Duke of Manchester.
1782-90. H. R. H. Henry Frederick, Duke of Cumberland.
1791-1812. H. R. H. George, Prince of Wales (George IV.).
1813-42. H. R. H. Augustus Frederick, Duke of Sussex.
1843-69. The Earl of Zetland, K.T.
1870-3. The Marquis of Ripon, K.G.
1874. H. R. H. Albert Edward, Prince of Wales, K.G., etc.

Men like these could not be frightened by papal anathemas or royal edicts; even the horrors of the Inquisition were impotent with men whose conscience said: Tyranny is wrong; oppose it at the risk of life, which is nothing compared with right! As shown by the previous list of eminent names, the English Masons elected the Grand Master of the Templars Grand Master of England's Masonry in 1154; hence they would not indorse the pope's murdering Templars, and breaking up their order from 1307 to 1314. Even Bossuet, in his "Abrégé de l'Histoire de France," says:

THE OBELISK AND FREEMASONRY. 107

"We know not whether there was more avarice and vengeance than justice in that execution."

In the preceding list are kings, princes, bishops, nobles, statesmen, savants, artists, and merchants; hence the theoretic and practical were represented and acted in concert. Such a continuity of a thousand years cannot be shown in any other country. We might trace Masonry in Scotland from Robert Bruce, A.D. 1314, to Albert Edward, Prince of Wales, 1880, but our epitome will not admit of it.

After such a chain of revered names invoked, from Tubalcain to Joseph and Solomon, and of great men elected, from Hiram Abif to Sir Christopher Wren, all that may be needed are a few Masonic celebrities from other countries.

ABSALOM, Bishop of Roschild. A society for mutual protection against the attacks of the pirates was established in the Isle of Zealand, Denmark, in the eighth century, and lasted till the sixteenth century of our era. The Danish Bishop was the founder of that useful order.

ST. BERNARD has been claimed by Brothers as a Mason, because he composed the rules for the Templars in the twelfth century. Also, his exhortation to soldiers of the Temple evinces knowledge of Masonry. He died 1153. He defeated the deification of the Virgin Mary, in his day. Pius IX. achieved it.

From the following movement of the Masonic associations on the Continent, it will appear that the architects, masons, and mechanics hitherto under papal patronage wished to be independent.

ERWIN VON STEINBACH, A.D. 1275, architect of the famous Strasburg Cathedral, convoked a congress of the Masonic associations and guilds at Strasburg A.D. 1275. We are told that this congress was attended by delegates from Germany, England, Italy, etc., and that the operative masons then and there assumed the name of *Freemasons*, and established new regulations for the government and guidance of their craft. Hence, the affix *free* dates back six centuries. This bold step soon attracted to the ranks of the *Freemasons* literati, scientists, inventors, and eminent men from all grades of society. Erwin von Steinbach, also the architect of the Cathedral of Cologne, became the Grand Master of German Masonry. He died A.D. 1318. To him German architects have ever pointed with pride; he was the Luther of their craft. The alchemists, inventors, and Rosicrucians, who were persecuted by the Inquisition as magicians and sorcerers, flocked to this liberal institution. We cannot help joining with *Erwin von Steinbach* the name of *Imhotep-Ur-Se-Phtah* (*Imhotep, the great—son of Phtah*), architect of the monuments at Denderah, lately translated from hieroglyphs on those ancient edifices.

TEMPLARS, A.D. 1118. This order was founded in 1118 and sanctioned by the church 1128, and was an outgrowth of the Crusades. Its founders were knights, who were a noble set of men for that period. Scotch Masonry has ever revered this name, and one of the principal Scotch orders has it now. H. R. H. Albert Edward, Prince of Wales, is its Grand Master. As previously mentioned the famous order of Templars was suppressed by Philippe le Bel, at the instigation of Pope Clement V., 1314, and its Grand Master, Molay, and many of his Brothers were burned at the stake. The bait for these murders was the wealth of this order, which the covetous pope and French king divided; but neither of them lived a year to enjoy the plunder. It is said the dying Grand Master summoned both before God's tribunal, and both died within a year.

HOSPITALLERS, or Knights of St. John, Teutonic Knights,

Knights of Rhodes, Knights of Malta. We will add here what the Crusades did for medieval progress and Masonry, of which many orders were created with the sanction of the church; and their names exist now, more or less modified: "Different nations marching, camping, and fighting together, began to lose some of their national prejudices; the middle and lower classes, and even nobles, princes, kings, and emperors, became more or less mixed and acquainted. An international feeling of mutual respect sprang up, which tended toward concord. New devices and mechanisms were seen and brought home from the East. The queens, princesses, and other ladies who accompanied the Crusaders, gave a tone of refinement that has ever since pervaded European idioms and manners. The knights were bound by a solemn oath to protect the fair sex, and to rescue widows and orphans from oppression," * whence the sublime idea of caring for the bereft widows and children of departed Brothers, the noblest emotion that ever entered man's breast.

ROSICRUCIANS. Here we must not omit the Rosicrucians,† who had their main strength in Germany, but had ramifications all over the globe. Their great learning and erudition gave them much influence during the Dark Ages and medieval times. The Rosicrucians have been traced to Ormus, who, about A.D. 46, founded an order that wore a red cross and were thence styled Rosicrucians. Ormus has been considered as a convert of St. Mark, the Evangelist. We are told they were joined by the learned order of the Essenes. The Knights Templars seem to have borrowed the red cross from the Eastern and West-

---

* See our "Origin, Progress, and Destiny of the English Language and Literature," p. 210.

† See the able article on this order by Charles Sotheran, 33°, in "Isis Unveiled," vol. II., p. 388.

ern Rosicrucians, so that this badge dates from A.D. 46 to our day. We give a short list of the celebrities claimed by this order:

AVICENNA, the famous Persian physician and author of many learned works on chemistry, A.D. 1030.

ALBERTUS MAGNUS. This bishop and architect wrote a system of symbolism cherished by Freemasons. He is also regarded as the founder of Gothic architecture, and as the author of a new set of laws for the operative masons about the time of the Strasburg Congress. He died A.D. 1280.

PARACELSUS was probably the most learned of German Rosicrucians, both as a physician and mystic. He wrote numerous books on the medicine and chemistry of his period. He was professor of Medicine at the University of Basle, A.D. 1526.

ROBERT FLUDD was in England what Paracelsus was in Germany. He was the great Rosicrucian in the British Isles. His books are on the occult sciences; some critics praise them, others pronounce them visionary. He florished about A.D. 1600.

BATTISTA PORTA was the Italian representative of Rosicrucianism, about 1605. He was the founder of the Academy of Secrets at Rome, whose meetings were interdicted by the pope. Yet he merely taught physical science; for to him we owe the *camera obscura*, the improvement in lenses. His treatise on Perspective, Botany, Physiognomy, Optics, and Natural Magic have ever been favorites with scholars and scientists. Thus had Rosicrucianism great intellects, extending from Britain to Persia. We might add other Rosicrucian names, but let these suffice.

BENJAMIN FRANKLIN became an initiate of Freemasonry about 1730, and Grand Master of Pennsylvania, 1734. He was an active Mason all his life, for he was present when Voltaire was initiated in France, 1778.

FREDERICK THE GREAT, King of Prussia, was initiated at

THE OBELISK AND FREEMASONRY. 111

Brunswick, 1738, and was patron and protector of
the craft all his life, when other sovereigns, at the
instigation of the Church, persecuted it.

GEORGE WASHINGTON was initiated at Fredericksburg, 1752,
and became Master Mason, 1753.

GENERAL JOSEPH WARREN, the Bunker Hill hero, was the
first Grand Master of the Massachusetts Lodge, 1769.

LESSING, author of "Nathan the Wise" and of "Fables,"
was a Brother of the Magic Tie about 1770. He
may be considered as the father of modern German
literature.

LALANDE, the great French astronomer, was an eminent
member of the Order of the Nine Sisters about
1776.

VOLTAIRE became an initiate of the Nine Sisters in 1778,
in the presence of Ben. Franklin, Lalande, Count de
Gebelin, and other celebrities. It was a grand occasion to see the great literatus join the ancient
Brotherhood, but the distinguished novice survived
his initiation only about three months.

GUSTAVUS III., King of Sweden, about 1777, established an
order, with rites and emblems taken from the Templars, Rosicrucians, and from French lodges. The
kings of Sweden are perpetual Grand Masters of the
craft.

GOETHE, the great German author and poet, was initiated
1780, and was an active member of the craft.

MARSHAL KELLERMANN, 33°, Duke of Valmy, who defeated
the allied armies under the Duke of Brunswick, 1792.

MESMER belonged to the "*Fratres Lucis*" about 1800.

SWEDENBORG joined the Brotherhood at Lund, 1806.

DE WITT CLINTON, the great engineer of the Erie Canal,
was initiated 1793, and became General Grand High
Priest of the General Chapter of the United States,
1816.

POPE PIUS IX. was initiated, it is said, into the mysteries of
the Masonic fraternity when young, but when Pope,

1865, he addressed to his Masonic brethren an allocution. He might easily have imitated his illustrious predecessor, Boniface IV., who issued that liberal diploma to the operative masons a thousand years before; but when Pius IX. grew old his courage failed him, and he tried to scold the companions of his youth. Thus the ubiquitous Masonic institution numbered kings, hierophants, popes, and presidents.

With such a galaxy of great intellects, from Tubalcain to Sir Christopher Wren, and from Rameses the Great to Washington, we cannot feel surprised, that Masonry, under various names and forms, but with the same spirit of mutual protection and charity, braved time, space, persecution, fire and sword, over six thousand years, and is now more vigorous than ever; whereas vast and powerful empires crumbled and vanished all along its quiet and peaceful pathway. We hope, after this splendid array of historic celebrities and monuments, Brethren will not feel like saying, that Masonry only dates to the Dark Ages or to the Revival of A.D. 1717, and is but of yesterday; for directly and indirectly it is connected with all that protohistory and history have noblest and most inspiring. Yet, since the discussion about the signs, emblems, and symbols on the American obelisk began, we read letters from Masons, who consciously or unconsciously seem to isolate Freemasonry, and give an impression, that it is rather a recent institution. If so, why invoke antediluvian and postdiluvian celebrities like Seth, Melchizedeck, Solomon, Pythagoras, etc. ?

The authors of some of the letters, that lately appeared in the Press seemed to make Masonry appear like some shadowy thing, as it was when, about 1738, popes began to anathematize and kings to proscribe Freemasonry. Moreover, they give the world an impression as though ancestry, pedigree, and stability were of little or no consequence, and as though a mere upstart or parvenu was as good as a veteran. Yet, an individual, association, family, or nation that can stand on an eminence and point to a glorious past, may look to the present with pride and to the future with confidence. Had these worthy Masons pointed to any number of the celebrities, whom the Brethren invoke in their Masonic rites and ceremonies, from Enoch and Joseph to Zoroaster and Plato, and told their colleagues such were our illustrious predecessors in antiquity and during the Middle Ages—such should we be now and in the future—they could not be considered as Freemasonry's magnifiers; whereas, in what they did tell them, they may justly be called Freemasonry's belittlers.

These Masonic radicals seem to forget, that the Masonic Brethren of to-day cherish, not only the perpendicular, square, compass, plummet, oblong, and even the magic number seven, etc., but that they utter names and words which, like those tools, date to remote antiquity. The kings, hierophants, and architects who planned, and the operative masons who reared Babel, the Pyramids, Parthenon, etc., may not have invoked Hiram, Solomon, etc., but they had analogous names of revered ancestors. The Egyptian Brethren may not have called their doorkeeper by a name, that had reference to the roof or foundation; yet they had such an officer, as may be realized by glancing at the entrances of the different mystery chambers in the Seti and Rameses Temple, discovered by Belzoni, 1818. They, no doubt, had grand masters, wardens, guides, candidates, as may be noticed by the groupings; their names may not have been pronounced or written like ours, but what of that?—the substance of the institution was there. This galaxy of great intellects, from Tubalcain to Franklin, conclusively proves that Freemasonry is not of yesterday or to-day, of Egypt or America, but of all times and of all countries.

To convince the Masonic fraternity that there ever has been a connection between ancient Oriental and modern Occidental Masonry, we translate a passage from Eliphas Lévi's *Dogme et Rituel de la Haute Magie*, 1861, vol. I., p. 338:

" The definitive alliance of reason and faith will result, not from their absolute distinction and separation, but from their mutual control and fraternal concourse. Such is the meaning of the two *columns* of Solomon's Porch, one of which is called *Jachin* * and the other *Boaz*,† one of which is *white* and the other *black*. They are distinct and separate; they are even contrary in appearance; but, if blind force attempted to unite them in bringing them together, the arch of the temple would crumble; for, separate, they have one and the same force; united, they are two forces, which destroy each other mutually."

This gives a glimpse of the emblems and symbols of the primitive Magi and Sages, whose science has been called, after them, *Magic*. The Chaldean, Assyrian, Persian, Egyptian, Hindu, Chinese, Greek, Roman, and Celtic magnates and hierophants shared similar symbols, from the building of the Tower of Babel to the Masonic Temple of New York City. The perusal of Lévi's erudite work would furnish to the members of the Magic Tie new ideas concerning their craft.

---

* The Hebrew of this term signifies, "*he shall establish.*"
† The Hebrew of this term signifies, "*fleetness, strength.*"

CHAPTER XIV.

"Freemasonry a purely moral and charitable order."—HYNEMAN.

WE read Dr. Rawson's interesting article on the Druzes in "Isis Unveiled," vol. II., pp. 313-315, and when we commenced to write this epitome, we asked him the favor to give us an article on some other Oriental order he might have seen during his tour over Egypt, Arabia, Palestine, and Syria. He magnanimously answered the favor we asked by giving us the following article on "Arab Masonry," which will be a valuable addendum to our long list of celebrities, and may be novel to many of the Masonic Brethren.

ARAB MASONRY.

"I had been told by an Egyptian poet and scholar, that the Arabs anciently worshiped the sun, and that their Masonry was a relic of that cult. This could hardly be true, since the sun is called *she* and the moon *he* among them, and no she could ever have been master in a lodge or shayk of a tribe. The master represents the unknown, the unseen, the all-powerful, and sits in the place of honor, whence he delivers his orders to his assistants, who are appointed at the time of the meeting.

"The candidate is prepared—partly clothed—and after a strict examination, under the direction of the master, is led before him, screened from the assembly by a vail or shawl held up by two brothers. The usual requirements as to age, free birth, and free will are made, and also touching his general knowledge of men and things, as is the case in an examination for a literary degree among us. Not a word is said about any religious faith or creed, not even as to belief in deity. It is presumed, that all rational men have a consciousness of a supreme existence, whether it is defined in words or symbols or not. The very word Allah (God) is an exotic in Arabia. The Bedawin idealizes the race, and imagines it personified into what he calls the Abram, the Great Father, usually written, among us, Abraham, and from whom are derived all living men, and to whom they all return at death. The only world of being they know is the present, and the only things worth notice are those relating to man. Their Masonry is, therefore, a means of securing a better life here, without any reference to any other, past or future. The idea of the collective man—humanity—is very ancient, and its teachings are simple, that man was derived from the great source, that he returns to the same, and that his duty is to make this life as important as possible, first for himself, which means, with the Arab, a discharge of duty to others for the sake of its return to himself.

"The will of the shayk (master) is the law of the lodge, but the will of the master must be guided by the ancient law, which is invariable and inevitable. The teachings of the lodge enlighten the conscience and lift the neophyte above himself into a prevision of motives, the only sure guaranty of morals. The notion—which has grown into a belief—that an injury done to any member of the race, will reflect upon the doer of the deed, not as an accident, but as a necessity of law—is a law of nature. Learning chiefly through observation, the Arab sees, in the frequent exercise of the will of the shayk, an apparent check or interference with the law of nature; but experience teaches him, through more careful observation, that the law invariably reasserts itself.

"The Abraham is the ideal of excellence in human life, the type that the initiated is instructed to imitate in the daily walk of life.

THE OBELISK AND FREEMASONRY. 117

"The esoteric work of the lodge would be out of place here, and intelligible to only a few initiates. A general idea, therefore, of the objects or purposes of the lodge will be more acceptable to the reader. The ceremony in the case of a poor man is often completed in an hour, while in that of a wealthy one it may continue during parts of three or five days, with agreeable interruptions in the way of feasts and entertainments, such as music, games, and recitations of the poets.

"The traditions of the lodge are and always have been oral, and there are no records in writing. The Arab looks upon writing as the enemy of memory, producing decay and final loss. It is difficult for us, who are trained to rely on books, to accept without hesitation the unwritten legends and traditions of the Orientals. But they say men make books to suit the hour and the interests of the passing moment, while antiquity made tradition, in which there can be no mixture of present interest, except for its preservation.

"One of the leading tenets in the lodge is, that the brotherhood owe to humanity an effort to make this life better, and to relieve humanity from the ills that obscure it, such as deceit, treachery, and ignorance, by inculcating truth, fidelity, and knowledge.

"The ceremonial is not extensive, when compared with ours, especially that of the Scottish rite (A. A. S. R.), but it teaches in its lessons, that the noblest object in life is to strive to become worthy of a first place for duty done, always subordinating the material to the spiritual, producing harmony by submission to the will of the master, who directs, and supervises all affairs in the lodge. The Arabs never were, and are not now, a nation in our sense of that term. Each tribe is independent of all others, alliances only excepted. There is no government over all the tribes, nor over any great number by any one person. Two or three are often found acting under the leadership of one shayk, but only for some specific purpose, and the alliance ends when that is accomplished. So also there is no grand lodge. Each lodge is supreme in itself. The Masonic brotherhood, therefore, is an aggregate of pebbles or gems, and is not a block of marble or granite. It is likened, by Arab poets, to a necklace of gems, engraved with the private marks of the greatest minds, held together by the golden chain of humanity.

" There is no community in the world, where charity and brotherly help, in time of need, are so sure as in that of the Bedawin, and none, in which imposture is sooner detected and punished. For three days the stranger, although he may be an enemy, or a murderer even, is entitled to and receives hospitality, including food, clothing, and shelter, and protection from harm, after which he must move on if in health, and in case of being an enemy or an outlaw, must defend himself. The grand sign is respected even on the battle-field, and there are many traditions of its use in saving the lives of noted persons.

" There is no Masonic literature in Arabia beyond the walls of the coast cities, and there is no true Masonry in those cities. The ritual, the whole framework of the craft in the cities, has become Europeanized more or less, according to the locality, as having been the abode of merchants and others from Europe. The true Arab Mason never records anything, except in his memory. There can be no paper brother among them, no book Mason, and, to advance, the neophyte must have knowledge obtained from authorized sources.

"Masonry in the desert is the privilege of the few. None but the choicest men are admitted to the charmed circle. To a stranger in such a country Masonic knowledge is an unequaled passport and introduction. An interesting feature of the craft is this: when one proposes a journey through a disturbed and therefore dangerous district, some trusty brother is selected to whom the traveler is delivered, and the masonic tie is renewed between them, when the guardian becomes responsible for his ward, life for life. This custom never fails of commanding respect, even between hostile tribes, except the traveler be guilty of shedding blood not in self-defence. The protection of women and children is an obligation that is never neglected. Any shortcoming in this matter would heap dishonor on the head of the erring one.

"To recount the whole catalogue of Masonic virtues, as practised on the desert, would fill a volume, and is not required here. My intention is to show the differences between Eastern and Western Masonry—that while there are some things in common, there are more peculiar to each section. Literature has changed the character of our craft in so many points, that careful study is required to ascertain the ancient meaning and practice, and even the closest application sometimes fails in tracing an ancient origin for some things in frequent use in the lodge and elsewhere by the brethren. No such innovation (removal of ancient landmarks) is possible in the desert, where the traditions of all the tribal lodges correct the errors, that may have crept in through some over-zealous worker.

"The language in use in the lodge is not that of the merchant of modern literature, but is that of the early ages, known as of Yoktan, in the centre; of Ishmael, in the west; of Yemen, in the south. The oldest known language that has been preserved is poetic. The ritual of the modern lodge is rhymed, question and answer, in the choicest terms, according to the grammar of the purest idiom, which is also the oldest. To the philologists these items are proofs of the antiquity of the order, more convincing even than monuments of stone, which can be made in every age, while language must grow and is not made. The Egyptians recorded in writing and in pictures their rites and ceremonies, which make visible the condition of the order in those matters at that time, about 4000 years ago. We read in those pictures the same lessons that are taught to us now, although they are distributed through the several degrees from the first to the thirty-second. The work in the Arab lodge shows a close connection between the members of the ancient brotherhoods of Egypt and Arabia, and also establishes the antiquity of the origin of the Bedawin lodges. There is not a word in use in the modern lodge, that has any reference to recent discoveries in science, or to the political or religious changes of the last twenty centuries. Neither Christ nor Mohammed are mentioned. This fact opens a charming vista to the antiquarian and philologist. The cost of an indulgence in this storehouse of antiquity is a local residence among the Bedawin Arabs, and a thorough knowledge of their language and customs.

"With the Arab the instruction of the lodge is a preparation for a better life; with the ancient Egyptians it was a preparation for death. The Arab still lives in the same social condition, in which history noticed him forty centuries ago, while the Egyptian ceased to exist as a nation about twenty-five centuries since. How much these different results were due to their peculiar ideas is yet an unsolved problem. The Arab has few wants, and is satisfied in their gratification; we have many, a great number of wants which have increased with our civilization, and the gratification of these does not bring content and rest, but stimulates to new endeavors. This unrest appears as well in the Masonic order, where one ritual after another surprises and bewilders all excepting their inventors. Whether this is for the permanent good of the craft is not yet determined, but is an open question.

"Whatever the Greek mysteries were, they have no modern type in the Arab lodge. The Greeks learned from the Egyptians, but despised the barbarian Arab. Their Masonic is also dead with their national system. It is probable that a dilution with religion killed it. Religious ideas are weakening the order in the United States, and a complete secularization is its only salvation. Secularism is stability and life, while religion is the mother of strife, change, decay, and death. Arab Masonry furnishes a beautiful emblem of eternity, whose cycles are marked by supreme efforts for the redemption of mankind from the slavery of ignorance and superstition, while the craft, in our day, lends itself for the perpetuation of errors peculiar to priestcraft.

"The ritual of the Arab is free from the antiquated absurdities, which are so brutal and shocking, *on paper*, and mere child's play in the work of our lodge, and in their place are found the real penalties, that can be inflicted on the apostate, chiefly social ostracism. Here is another evidence of the antiquity of the order in that locality, since in this age blood-feuds have apparently led to an undervaluation of human life in the Orient, and if the order was modern we should expect to see penalties threatened and inflicted, that were in unison with the spirit of the age—say from the sixth century to the present."

As Dr. Rawson's essay speaks for itself, he being an eminent Mason, it needs no comment from us.

That mysterious Asiatic peninsula, called Arabia, ever seemed to us a geographic, historic, and political wonder; for, while empires like Assyria, Persia, Egypt, India, Greece, and Rome were changing and vanishing, Arabia and Ishmael's children remained immutable. The Assyrians, Persians, Egyptians, Greeks, and Romans tried in vain to subjugate Hagar's progeny; they stand to-day, with their language, customs, manners, and traditions, where they stood ages ago. Renan and Maspéro have lately given the world some valuable hints on that mysterious people and country. Perhaps Freemasonry, with its gentle, peaceful, and persuasive methods of approaching peoples, will succeed in opening that sealed country to the world; if so, Dr. Rawson will be considered as a pioneer in the grand enterprise.

CHAPTER XV.

"In Egypt obelisks were called the rays of the sun."—SHAUBERG.

As readers may on this occasion feel an interest in the many obelisks, that were carried from Egypt to Italy, Constantinople, France, England, and Germany, we give an account of them, with anecdotes connected with some of them. The Roman Emperors, from Augustus to Adrian, vied in adorning their capital with Egyptian obelisks.

H. The obelisk standing in the *Piazza of St. Peter* * at Rome was brought from Egypt, under Caligula, about A.D. 38, and erected in the Vatican Circus, whence it was transferred to the place, which it now occupies, by the great engineer Fontana, whose plan was considered the best among the five hundred submitted to Pope Sixtus V., A.D. 1585. In its removal Fontana employed several hundred workmen, many horses, and very complex machinery. His success was considered almost a miracle.

---

* It has been claimed that this monolith is one of the two thus mentioned by Herodotus (B. II., 111): "Pheron sent to the Temple of the Sun two obelisks, too remarkable to be unnoticed. Each was formed of one solid stone, 100 cubits (150 feet) high, and 8 cubits (12 feet) broad." Concerning this obelisk, Pliny says: "The third obelisk at Rome is in the Vatican Circus, which was constructed by the Emperors Caius and Nero; this being the only one of them all, that was broken in the carriage. Nuncoreus, the son of Sesosis, made it, and there remains another by him, 100 cubits high, which, by order of an oracle, he consecrated to the sun, after having lost his sight and recovered it." This seems to corroborate the statement of Herodotus.

THE OBELISK AND FREEMASONRY. 123

Whole height............................	132 ft. 2 in.
Without pedestal, ornament on top, etc......	82 ft. 9 in.
Base lines of shaft.......................	8 ft. 10 in.
Mass or volume..................	about 4,400 cubic feet.

This monolith, bearing no hieroglyphs, is a blank for hieroglyphic decipherers. On one side is engraved a dedication to Augustus; on another a dedication to Tiberius. It is of *rose-colored granite*, composed of quartz, felspar, and hornblende, found in the quarry of *Syene*, in Upper Egypt, whence Egyptian engineering and mechanic skill transported such heavy masses to all parts of the country. Thence this beautiful stone has been called *syenite*.

III. The obelisk in front of the church of *Santa Maria Maggiore* is one of the two, that adorned the tomb of Augustus.' Mercati thinks the two were erected there by Claudius as a tribute of gratitude. Its twin now adorns Monte Cavallo. It is of rose-colored *syenite*.

Whole height.................................	89 ft.
Without pedestal (only the shaft)..................	49 ft.

No hieroglyphics; broken in three pieces.

Pope Sixtus V. had it transferred from Augustus' tomb, under the supervision of Fontana, to where it now stands, A.D. 1587. To the erection of this obelisk belongs the well known anecdote of the man who, in the midst of the silence imposed, under penalty of death, by the first of the absolute pontiffs, saved the compromised operation by calling to Fontana, "*Acqua alle funi*" (wet the ropes). This spectator was a coaster of the Genoese Riviera, named *Bresca*. He obtained for his reward permission to fly the papal flag at his mast and the hereditary privilege of supplying the Apostolic palace with palm-leaves on Palm Sunday.

IV. The obelisk before the church of *St. John Lateran*, it is said, was originally at Thebes, whence it was transferred to Alexandria by the order of Constantine, who destined it to adorn Byzantium; but his son, Constantius, had it carried to Rome and erected in the centre of the *spina*, on the Circus Maximus, about A.D. 357. It was found A.D. 1587, under débris sixteen feet deep, *broken in three pieces.*

Pope Sixtus V. had it removed to where it now is by Fontana, A.D. 1588.

Whole height............................ 150 ft.
Without base, etc., only its shaft........... 106 "
Base lines of shaft............. 9 ft. 8 in. : 9 ft. 10 in.
Weight................................ 445 tons.

This monument bears hieroglyphic inscriptions, that have been translated by Dr. Birch. They seem to be in honor of Thothmes III., who, as Egyptian records show, erected many beautiful obelisks in various cities of his dominions about 1762 B.C. It bears the royal signets of Thothmes III. and Thothmes IV., and is of rose-colored *syenite*, a shade more grayish than the others. It is the largest obelisk now known, although Fontana had to cut off a part of the lower end of the shaft on account of its being fractured. When and how these grand monuments were overthrown we know not. Some think they were, in the course of time, struck by lightning. We are told this one was overthrown by the barbarians and broken in three pieces.

V. The obelisk known as the *Flaminian* obelisk, at *Porta del Popolo*, was transported from Egypt to Rome under Octavius Augustus, about 20 B.C. Late discoveries and hieroglyphic translations indicate, that it dates to Pharaoh Seti I., father of Rameses II. It was found in three pieces under the ruins of the Circus Maximus. It had to be shortened on account of its fractures. This obelisk attracted more attention than any one of the others. In its hieroglyphic inscription occur the names of Seti and Rameses. Sixtus V., who seemed determined to adorn the Pontifical City, had it transferred to, and erected on, the site it now occupies, by the illustrious Fontana, A.D. 1589.

THE OBELISK AND FREEMASONRY. 125

Whole height.............................. 116 ft.
Without pedestal (only the shaft)............ 78 ft. 6 in.
Base lines of shaft........................ 8 ft. 5 in.

It bears hieroglyphic inscriptions, which have been translated into Greek by Hermapion, under the Roman Emperors, into English by Rev. G. Tomlinson, and into German by the veteran Egyptologist Seyffarth, who gave us the following interesting anecdote concerning this obelisk in a German pamphlet. We translate it into English:

"As early as 1826 I discovered, that the obelisk at Porta del Popolo is the one Hermapion (*apud* Ammian. Marc. XVII., 4) translated, but I was bound by a promise to keep silent till the work, undertaken by Pope Gregory XVI., was issued. Champollion, then also in Rome, had not been able to find Hermapion's obelisk, and assured me one day, that it must yet lie buried in some cellar (*sarà in una cantina*). Meanwhile, Champollion had promised to translate the inscriptions of the Flaminian and other obelisks, and to have its explanations printed in the forthcoming work. The tablets, ready 1826, were sent to Champollion in Paris, who was thenceforth occupied to translate the inscriptions; but he did not succeed. He died ten years after without having reached his object.

"Now, Rosellini in Florence, Champollion's pupil and friend, together with Ungarelli in Rome, were invited to undertake the translation of the inscriptions. The text was fully and correctly written in Ungarelli's '*Interpretatio* * *Obeliscorum Urbis*,' Rome, 1842. I myself compared and verified the tablets with the original under a good magnifying glass during my sojourn in Rome, before they were engraved, 1826.

"Champollion had only deciphered simple passages, which Ungarelli had printed in notes before Champollion. He

---

* Prof. Seyffarth considers Ungarelli's interpretations of the hieroglyphs unreliable.

also had no idea, that the obelisk near Porta del Popolo was the one translated by Hermapion. Now, Ungarelli was obliged to continue to translate and publish the text after Champollion's system, which was only accomplished in 1842, seventeen years after. When the book reached me, I immediately showed the agreement between Hermapion's version and the Flaminian obelisk, and did not neglect to draw attention to my key to the hieroglyphs and to the incorrectness of Champollion's system in various treatises in 1844 and 1845, etc. In our translation of the Flaminian obelisk we include Hermapion's Greek words, and Ungarelli's explanations after Champollion's system. *Ramses* and *Osymanthyas*, son and father, are identified, because, as Manetho teaches, they reigned contemporaneously. Osymandias, or probably Ossima-n-thewa, is Seso-s, Seso-htor, the well-known Sesostris, friend of Phtha. The two divinities, who speak here as ('we'), are the two Cabiri Sun (Horus-Ra) and Moon (Tamie), Day and Night, who produce all things through the Creator. The obelisk itself was, as the inscription indicates, erected by *Ramses*."

We add here an English translation of Hermapion's version of the hieroglyphs from Ammianus Marcellinus, B. XVII., c. 4, § 12:

"The first line, beginning on the south side, bears this interpretation: 'The Sun to Ramestes the King—I have given to thee to reign with joy over the whole earth: to thee, whom the Sun and Apollo love—to thee, the mighty truth-loving son of Heron—the god-born ruler of the habitable earth; whom the Sun has chosen above all men, the valiant, warlike King Ramestes. Under whose power, by his valor and might, the whole world is placed. The King Ramestes, the immortal son of the Sun.'

"The second line is: 'The mighty Apollo, who takes his stand upon truth, the lord of the diadem, he who has honored Egypt by becoming its master, adorning Heliopolis, and having created the rest of the world, and having greatly honored the gods, who have their shrines in the city of the Sun; whom the son loves.'

"The third line: 'The mighty Apollo, the all-brilliant son of the Sun, whom the Sun chose above all others, and to whom the valiant Mars gave gifts. Thou whose good fortune abideth for ever. Thou whom Ammon loves. Thou who hast filled the temple of the Phœnix with good things. Thou to whom the gods have given long life. Apollo, the mighty son of Heron, Ramestes the king of the world. Who has defended Egypt, having subdued the foreign enemy. Whom the Sun loves. To whom the gods have given long life—the master of the world—the immortal Ramestes.'

"Another second line: 'The Sun, the great God, the master of heaven. I have given unto thee a life free from satiety. Apollo, the mighty master of the diadem; to whom nothing is comparable. To whom the lord of Egypt has erected many statues in this kingdom. And has made the city of Heliopolis as brilliant as the Sun himself, the master of heaven. The son of the Sun, the king living for ever, has co-operated in the completion of this work.'

"A third line: 'I, the Sun, the god, the master of heaven, have given to Ramestes the king might and authority over all. Whom Apollo, the truth-lover, the master of time, and Vulcan, the father of the gods, hath chosen above others by reason of his courage. The all-rejoicing king, the son of the Sun, and beloved by the Sun.'

"The first line, looking toward the east: 'The great God of Heliopolis, the mighty Apollo who dwelleth in Heaven, the son of Heron whom the Sun hath guided. Whom the gods have honored. He who ruleth over all the earth: whom the Sun hath chosen before all others. The king valiant by the favor of Mars. Whom Ammon loveth, and the all-shining god who hath chosen him as a king for everlasting.' And so on."

This clearly shows that the pioneers in Egyptology, who were finding the key to the hieroglyphs, had difficulties to commence the decipherings; for there were then in Rome Champollion and his pupil Rosellini, Ungarelli, and Seyffarth, who were all trying their methods and keys to begin hieroglyphic translations. They had Hermapion's Greek version of one of the obelisks; but they knew not which it was, and had difficulty to find it, even with the aid of those indications.

To enable readers to realize some primary obstacles in the way of the new science, styled Egyptology, we translate what Mariette Pacha says in his *Aperçu de l'Histoire d'Egypte*, p. 189, concerning the famous " Rosetta Stone : " *

" Discovered, about 65 years ago, by French soldiers, who were digging entrenchments near Rosetta. The stone, which bears this name, was of the highest importance in Egyptian archeology. On its principal surface are engraved *three* inscriptions; the two first are in Egyptian, and written in the two writings current at that epoch. One is in hieroglyphic character, reserved for priests; it only contains fourteen lines, mutilated by fractures in the stone. The other is in cursive writing, principally used and understood by the people; † this numbers thirty-two lines of text. Finally, the third inscription on the stela is in Greek, and comprises fifty-four lines. The latter part of the monument, found at Rosetta, contains information of high interest. From the interpretation of the Greek text results a version of the preceding original transcript in the two Egyptian writings. Hence the Rosetta Stone gives us, in a perfectly known language (*Greek*), the translation of a text, conceived in another language not understood at the time, when the stela was discovered. Who, then, does not see the utility of this men-

---

* A slab of basalt, marked 24, in the British Museum, has engraved on it a *hieroglyphic, demotic*, and *Greek* inscription. This slab was thrown up among the rubbish while the French were digging trenches to fortify Rosetta, 1799. The English obtained it at the capitulation of Alexandria, 1801, among the articles collected by the French army. The French engineer Bouchard, or Broussard, first discovered it.

† Thence called *demotic* writing.

THE OBELISK AND FREEMASONRY.   129

tion? To ascend from the known to the unknown is not beyond the means of prudent criticism. Already we perceive that, if the Rosetta Stone acquired in science the celebrity it enjoys to-day, it is because it furnished the true key to that mysterious writing, whose secret Egypt had kept so long. However, we must not imagine that the deciphering of hieroglyphs by means of the Rosetta Stone was accomplished at the first trial, and without groping in the dark. On the contrary, the savants tried for twenty years without success. At last Champollion appeared. Prior to him people thought each of the letters, that compose hieroglyphic writing, was a *symbol;* namely, that in every single one of those letters was expressed a complete *idea.* The merit of Champollion consisted in proving, that Egyptian writing contains signs which express *sounds;* in other words, that it is *alphabetic.* He noticed that wherever in the Greek text the proper name of Ptolemy is met with, there may be found, at a corresponding place of the Egyptian text, a certain number of signs, enclosed within an elliptic space. From this he concluded: 1, That the names of kings were indicated, in the hieroglyphic system, by a sort of escutcheon, which he styled *cartouche;* 2, That the signs contained in that cartouche must be, letter for letter, the name of Ptolemy.

"Even supposing the vowels omitted, Champollion was already in possession of five letters: P, T, L, M, S. Again, Champollion knew, according to a second Greek inscription, engraved on an obelisk of Philæ, that on this obelisk a hieroglyphic cartouche is visible, which must be that of Cleopatra. If his first reading was correct, the P, the L, and the T, of Ptolemy, must be refound in the second proper name; but, at the same time, this second proper name furnished K and R. Although very imperfect, when applied to other cartouches, the alphabet, thus revealed to Champollion through the names of Cleopatra and Ptolemy, put him in possession of nearly all the other consonants.

"Thenceforth Champollion had no need to hesitate concerning the *pronunciation* of signs; for, from the day this proof was furnished, he could certify that he possessed the Egyptian alphabet. But now remained the language; for pronouncing words is nothing, if we know not what they mean. Here Champollion's genius could soar. He perceived that his alphabet, drawn from proper names and applied to words of the language, simply furnished *Coptic*. Now Coptic, in its turn, is a language which, without being as well explored as Greek, had for a long time not been less accessible. Therefore the veil was completely removed. The Egyptian language was only Coptic, written in hieroglyphs; or, to speak more correctly, Coptic is only the language of the ancient Pharaohs, written, as we previously stated, in Greek letters. The rest may be inferred. From sign to sign Champollion really proceeded from the known to the unknown, and soon the illustrious founder of Egyptology could lay the foundations of this beautiful science, which has for its object the interpretation of the *hieroglyphs*. Such is the Rosetta stone."

We introduce this graphic and simple passage to show the elements of a science that lights the path to the primitive history of our race. *Cuneiform* inscriptions and decipherings were but a logic sequence to Egyptian hieroglyphs. Now ancient American signs, emblems, symbols, and characters should be carefully collected, compared, and studied, so as to see how they may, in remote ages, have been connected with similar characters in the old world.

When those English, French, German, and Italian Egyptologists vied in efforts to discover and contrive a key to the hieroglyphs, the taste and desire for Egyptian obelisks revived; and about A.D. 1818 France and England wished to see some of those graceful Egyptian pillars in their capitals; and now Americans are anxious to have an obelisk in their metropolis. Next the fatherland will try to obtain and transfer one to Berlin.

VI. The monolith in the Piazza Navona was removed

from the Circus of Caracalla to where it now stands by order of Pope Innocent X., under the direction of the engineer Bernini, A.D. 1651.

Whole height............................. 99 ft.
Without pedestal (only the shaft) .... 54 ft.
Base lines of the shaft..................... 4 ft. 5 in.

Its hieroglyphic inscriptions contain deifying names, applied to the vain Domitian, who had it quarried in Egypt, whence it was brought to Rome, about A.D. 90. It has a fountain round its base, and is sometimes styled "Pamphilian obelisk."

VII. The obelisk of Piazza della Minerva has for its pedestal a poorly-contrived elephant of marble, the work of Bernini, whose eminent predecessor would not have been guilty of such an artistic solecism. No wonder it affixed to Bernini the nickname of "*The Elephant*." It was erected under Pope Alexander VII., A.D. 1667.

Whole height................................ 40 ft.
Without pedestal (only the shaft)................ 17 ft.

It bears hieroglyphic inscriptions.

VIII. The obelisk of *Mahuteo della Rotunda*, in front of the Pantheon of Agrippa, has, like that of the Piazza Navona, a fountain round its base. It was erected under Clement XL, 1711.

Whole height................................. 48 ft.
Without pedestal (only the shaft)................ 20 ft.

It has hieroglyphic inscriptions that mention Rameses II., whence its original erection in Egypt has been attributed to this great Pharoah, conqueror of the Khetas.

IX. The obelisk on *Quirinale del Monte Cavallo* appears

to be broken in two or three places. It was erected by Antinori during the Pontificate of Pius VI., 1786.

Whole height.................................. 95 ft.
Without base, etc. (only the shaft)............... 48 ft.

No hieroglyphics. Zoëga has a plate of it in his great work, No. 6.

X. The monolith before the church *Trinita del Monte* also was erected by Antinori, under Pius VI., 1789.

Whole height.................................. 100 ft.
Without pedestal (only the shaft)............about 43 ft.

Bears hieroglyphics. Zoëga represents it by plate 7.

Archeologists say this monument was carried to Rome by Sallustianus Crispus, prefect of Numidia, and erected in the gardens of Sallust during the reign of Vespasian, A.D. 69–79. Hence it was called Sallustian Obelisk. It is supposed it arrived in Rome without hieroglyphs, and that those now on it were copied from the *Flaminian* obelisk.

XI. The obelisk on *Monte Citorio* was brought to Rome under Octavius Augustus, about 20 B.C., and raised in Campus Martius by the mathematician, Facundus Novus, who so adjusted it as to serve for a *gnomon*,* or style, to indicate the hours of the day on a dial, drawn on the pavement. A.D. 1748 it was found buried and was unearthed. Under

---

* Herodotus tells us (B. II., 109) : "As to the pole, or *gnomon*, and the division of the day into twelve parts, the Greeks received them from the Babylonians." Here we realize that not only the Egyptians, but the Greeks and Romans derived knowledge from *Assyria*. Palladius Rutilius, who lived about A.D. 350, has in his book "*De Re Rustica*," at the end of every month, a table, showing the correspondence of the divisions of the day to the different lengths of the *gnomon*. Clocks were then among the unknown things, and watches were in the vocative as late as A.D. 1477.

Pius VI., A.D. 1792, it was transferred to, and erected in, the place it now occupies, by Antinori.

Whole height..................................... 110 ft.
Without pedestal (only the shaft)................ 72 ft.

It has hieroglyphic inscriptions. Zoëga shows it in plate 8. It is of rose-colored *syenite*, and stands on a pedestal of the same stone. This beautiful monolith is attributed to *Psammitichus* II., who had it erected at Heliopolis, from 594 to 588 B.C. Psammitichus I., grandfather of Psammitichus II., was the founder of the 26th Dynasty. He first invited Greeks to settle in Egypt. Herodotus (B. I., 105— B. II., 2, 28, 30, 151—161) has much to say about Psammitichus I. and his son Nekos, father of Psammitichus II., whom Greek ambassadors came to consult concerning the Olympic Games. This obelisk has also been ascribed to Rameses II., or Sesostris; but this must be an error, for Psammitichus' name has been deciphered from its hieroglyphs. The Father of History tells us (B. I., 105): "The Scythians, having obtained the entire possession of Asia, advanced toward Egypt. Psammitichus, King of Egypt, met them in Palestine of Syria, and, by presents and importunity united, prevailed on them to return." This event, together with the Greek ambassadors, make Psammitichus a historic landmark for archeologists. We cannot help recording here what Pliny says: "The obelisk, erected in the Campus Martius, has been applied to a singular purpose by the late Emperor Augustus: that of marking the shadows projected by the sun, and so measuring the length of the days and nights. With this object a stone pavement was laid, the extreme length of which corresponded exactly with the length of the shadow thrown by the obelisk at the sixth hour on the day of the winter solstice. After this period the shadow would go on, day by day, gradually decreasing, and then again would as gradually increase, correspondingly with certain lines of brass, that were inserted in the stone—a device well deserving to be known, and due to the ingenuity of Facundus Novus, the mathematician."

This was two millenniums ago, when not every man, woman, and child had a gold or silver watch in his, her, or its pocket; aye, not even the great Augustus had a watch or a clock in his palaces!

XII. The obelisk on *Monte Pincio* was found, A.D. 1633, in the Circus Varianus, outside of the walls of Rome. Zoëga calls it the *Barberini Obelisk*, of which he says: " Hic e Romanis obeliscis adhuc cognitis solus expectat sospitatorem." * A.D. 1823, pope Pius VII. had it transferred to the spot it now occupies.

Whole height.................................. 57 ft.
Without pedestal (only the shaft)................. 31 ft.

It bears hieroglyphs, which have been translated by several Egyptologists. This is the latest of the obelisks with hieroglyphs; on it occur the names of the emperor Adrian, the empress Sabina, and their adopted son and favorite, *Antinous*. As the occasion of this obelisk was touching and tragic, we relate it: Antinous was born in Bithynia; when he appeared at court the emperor and empress were struck with his beauty and adopted him as heir to the throne. Wherever Adrian and Sabina traveled Antinous accompanied them. While in Egypt Adrian consulted the oracle of Beza, who told him danger threatened him, unless a person very dear to him was immolated for his preservation. When Antinous heard of it, he jumped into the Nile and drowned himself. Adrian wept and ordered mourning throughout the empire, and employed all the eminent artists to preserve and perpetuate the beauty and graces of the departed. Temples were built, a priesthood

---

* " Of the Roman obelisks now known, this alone awaits a savior." When the great Danish archeologist wrote this in Rome, A.D. 1797, this obelisk must have been in an abandoned condition.

established, statues raised, medals were struck, and a magnificent city was founded on the site of Beza, where the sad catastrophe happened; and that city was called *Antinoöpolis*. Such was the occasion of the obelisk that now graces *Monte Pincio*, at Rome. In the translation of its hieroglyphs we read: "Hadrianus, the ever-living, I give thee glory, which thy heart loves, etc. . . . The chief of the South and North, being the great Lord of every country, etc. . . . Sabina of life and health established, Augusta the ever-living, etc. . . . Antinous is justified as a spirit, etc. . . . He has been adored by workmen of Thoth, etc. . . . Spiritualized as a spirit at rest within the limits of the countries, etc. . . . He has been recognized as a god in the divine places of Egypt, which have been founded for him, etc. . . . Likewise they gave the title of a city to his name," etc.

This monolith shows these historic facts: that the ancient Egyptian hieroglyphs and language (*Coptic*) withstood Persian, Greek, and Latin conquest and rule; and that as late as Adrian, A.D. 132, obelisks and hieroglyphic inscriptions were in vogue among the Roman magnates. Several statues of the famous Antinous, recorded on this obelisk, are now in the Paris Museum. History severely censures Adrian for showering imperial favors on a dazzled youth, and then consulting and listening to silly oracles.

When tourists pass up the Nile and reach the town of *Esne*, let them remember, while visiting the ancient ruins, that there occurred the tragic death of Antinous, whose memory was perpetuated by the obelisk of Monte Pincio, which has since caused many sentimental emotions.

XIII. An obelisk that adorned the *Circus of Flora* at Rome was carried to Florence, and erected in the Boboli Gardens of the city, adorned and rendered famous by the Medici.

XIV. The obelisk of the *Villa Mattei*, which formerly graced the Ara Cœli of the Capitol, was transferred in 1817 to the site it now occupies. It is a small fragment of a real Egyptian obelisk, mounted on a pedestal of ordinary granite.

Height.................................. 8 ft. 3 in.

It bears hieroglyphs that mention the famous *Rameses II.*, to whom its original erection is ascribed.

XV. To vie with Rome, the citizens of Catana, in Sicily, erected an obelisk in front of their cathedral. This monument differs from those at Rome in being polygonal instead of quadrilateral; but, like that of Della Minerva at Rome, it is placed on the back of an elephant, raised on a pedestal. It is considered Egyptian. We read in Larousse's "Dictionnaire Universel du XIX. Siècle," just issued, that *Cortona*, Velletri, etc., had obelisks standing in their squares during Roman sway, for some of their débris have been found.

XVI. The ancient Samnite city, *Beneventum*, has among its rich remains an Egyptian obelisk.

Height.................................... 9 ft.

XVII. *The obelisk of Arles*, in Provence, France, after having adorned the spina of the Circus, was overthrown and remained in the mire of the Rhone, whence it was taken and erected in the *Place Royale*, A.D. 1676. Some archeologists consider it of Egyptian workmanship; others tell us the granite, of which it is formed, came from the quarries of Esterel, or from those in Corsica. Some Latin authors call Arles *Arelatum*, others *Arelate*, and poets *Arelas*. Strabo speaks of it as a commercial emporium; Mela mentions it as the richest city in Gallia Narbonensis. It became the residence of some of the Emperors, who, wishing to give to Arelatum some of the prestige of Rome, adorned it with an obelisk and circus. Perhaps this monolith was brought from Egypt, but history is silent on the subject.

Height.................................. about 50 ft.

Without hieroglyphs. It would seem as though the Romans tried to imitate the Egyptian obelistic art, for it has been claimed that the obelisk of Catana, in Sicily, is not of Egyptian workmanship.

Such are a few of the votive pillars, transferred from Egypt to Rome and France. They had been raised to the sun god, *Ra*, and to the sun goddess, *Sati* (sunbeam), who were worshiped by the Egyptians as Nature's productive principle. Only eleven adorn Rome now, whereas a Roman author, called P. Victor, in an essay on the quarters of ancient Rome, mentions six large *obelisks* and forty-two smaller ones. The others may be found buried, like the *Lateran obelisk*. These mementos of primitive Oriental civilization attract travelers to and keep them at Rome. One of those monuments in New York will be an honor to the country, that already has cities in the great West, named after *Memphis* and *Cairo*. Thus do namesakes and patronymics indicate direct or indirect connection between individuals, families, tribes, nations, and races.

The Emperors of the East remembered the wishes of Constantine, who, as previously stated, desired to embellish Byzantium with Egyptian obelisks. Hence, Theodosius the Great had two of the votive monuments transferred from Egypt to Constantinople, about A.D. 390. Both were placed in the *Hippodrome*, now called *Almeidan*.

XVIII. The largest of the two still occupies the same spot. It is ascribed to Pharaoh Thothmes III.

Height .... 50 ft.

It bears hieroglyphs, translated by Dr. Birch, from whose notes we quote:

"He (Thothmes III.) made it a gift to his father, Amon-Ra, Lord of the foundations of the Earth. He has gone round the great waters of *Naharina*.* He has made his frontiers to the tips of the Earth, his seats to Naharina."

Gliddon, in his "Ancient Egypt," p. 64, corroborates the above when he speaks of "*conquests through Central Asia to Hindostan*" by Pharaohs of the Eighteenth Dynasty, mentioned by translations from the hieroglyphic " Tablet of *Abydos*, the Procession of the *Ramessium*, the Procession of *Medeenet-Haboo*, and the Tomb of *Gurnah*." Here the American savant refers to Thothmes III., whose queen *Amense* he mentions.

XIX. The smallest of the two was moved from the Hippodrome to the Gardens of the Seraglio, since the city of Constantinople was captured by the Turks, A.D. 1453.

Height..................................... 35 ft.
Base lines of shaft......................... 6 by 6 ft.

It bears hieroglyphs. This obelisk has been ascribed to a Pharaoh named Nectanebo I., who, according to Gliddon, was of the Thirtieth Dynasty, and reigned 377–359 B.C. Nectanebo was the last Egyptian king of the Egyptian race.

XX. One of the obelisks on the Isle of Philæ, in Upper Egypt found its way to England, 1818; an event, though scarcely known, which was the prelude to Egyptian collections and museums. This desire and taste soon spread to America, whither Abbott's collection went, and where Gliddon arose.

The *Philæ obelisk*, now at Corfe Castle, Dorsetshire, England, is a monolith:

Height, about.............................. 22 ft.
Base lines of the shaft..................... 2 ft. 2 in.
Top lines of the shaft...................... 1 ft. 6 in.

Hieroglyphs?
As this monument had such a romantic career, we men-

---
* Mesopotamia.

THE OBELISK AND FREEMASONRY. 139

tion some of its striking adventures. A Homer, Virgil, Valmiki, Firdousi, etc., might find material for an epic poem. Its royal projectors; the historic spot it occupied on the Nile; its removal from the *Isle of Philæ* to England, and the thrilling episodes connected therewith; its art-loving owner, its bold remover; and the new home it found on the green lawns at Corfe Castle—than which no more charming site could be found in the British Isles—may attract a Tennyson, Longfellow, or Lowell. No doubt, as soon as tourists know that such an ancient architectural gem adorns Corfe Castle, they will flock thither, and admire the classic taste of *Henry Bankes*, who endowed his residence, town, and country with a monument that saw the Nile glide along its base from 140 B.C. to A.D. 1818, and that now beholds the British Channel on the south, the Isle of Wight on the east, and Cornwall on the west.

We read that Ptolemy VII., surnamed Evergetes, and his queen Cleopatra, whose reign was much disturbed, erected several obelisks at Philæ, near which was the small rockbound Isle of *Abatos*, where Isis had built a tomb and deposited the remains of *Osiris*. Abatos means *inaccessible*, because only the Egyptian priests could visit that sacred island.

Henry Bankes, member of Parliament from 1780 to 1826, and author of "*Civil and Constitutional History of Rome*," after his arduous legislative and literary labors, visited Egypt in 1818, and obtained, through the British consul, from the Pasha, permission to remove one of the obelisks of Philæ. *Belzoni* was then busily engaged in Egyptian explorations, and Mr. Bankes induced him to ascend the Nile with him, in order to remove the monolith to England. As Belzoni has written an interesting chapter on the subject in his "Researches and Operations in Egypt, Nubia," etc., pp. 321-349, we quote a few extracts therefrom:

» "On my arrival at Gournou, I found the consul, Mr. Salt,

Mr. *Bankes*, and Baron Sack had arrived from Cairo. At this period Mr. Bankes solicited me to ascend the Nile as far as the island of Philæ, to remove the obelisk I had taken possession of before, in the name of the British consul. The consul then informed me that he had ceded the said obelisk to Mr. Bankes, who intended to send it to England on his own account. I gladly accepted the undertaking, as I was pleased to have the opportunity of seeing another piece of antiquity on its way to England, and of obliging a gentleman for whom I had great regard.

"On the 16th of November, 1818, we left Thebes for the first cataract of the Nile. . . . On the 21st of November, 1818, we visited Eduu, and took a minute survey of those truly magnificent ruins, which are so covered with a profusion of objects that, if a traveler was to repeat his visits every day of his life, he might still find something new to be observed. . . . Next day the party arrived at Assouan, and I went to the island of Philæ to take a view of the bank where I was to embark the obelisk, and have it conveyed to the cataract, where it was to be launched. . . . I had some difficulty, at first, in removing the obelisk from its original station; but once put on its way, it soon came to the water-side. *The pedestal was rather more troublesome, owing to its square form.* It was almost buried under the rubbish, and as we had no tackle whatever, and very little wood, it retarded the work one or two days longer. There is no wood in those places, except what they procure from Cairo to repair their boats. . . .

"Our party prepared for their voyage to the second cataract. The obelisk was now ready to be embarked. . . . . The pier appeared strong enough to bear at least forty times the weight it had to support; but alas! when the obelisk came gradually on from the sloping bank, and all the weight rested on it, the pier, with the obelisk and some of the men, took a slow movement, and majestically descended into the river, wishing us better success. I was not three yards off when this happened, and for some minutes, I must confess,

I remained like a post. The first thing that came into my head was the loss of such a piece of antiquity, and the blame of the antiquarian republic in the world. . . . The laborers were of various humor; some went one way, some another, and I remained alone, seated on the bank, to contemplate the little part which projected out of the water, and the eddies made by the current on that spot, in consequence of the obelisk below. The effects of surprise did not last long. I began to reflect, and saw the possibility of taking the obelisk up again. . . . I found that the loss would only be two or three days' work. . . . Mr. Bankes was not there when this happened. . . . On his arrival he said: '*that such things would happen sometimes.*' . . . I informed him that the obelisk was not lost, and that in two or three days it would be on board. . . . The two next days were employed in this operation."

We might add that a band of ruffians, suborned by an Italian speculator, pointed pistols at Belzoni for removing the obelisk, and other dramatic incidents; but suffice it to say that Belzoni, Mr. Bankes, and his obelisk safely reached Rosetta, whence it was shipped to England, and that Belzoni started for the temple of Jupiter Ammon, in the western desert, April 20, 1819. Hence Belzoni and Henry Bankes, M.P., may truly be called the practical pioneers of modern monumental Egyptology; whereas Champollion and Rosellini, who explored Egypt in 1828, and laid the foundation for the great work styled "*Monuments of Egypt and Nubia,*" etc., published by the French government, 1835–1845, must be considered as theoretical pioneers. Moreover, while Belzoni was occupied at the obelisk, Bankes discovered the inscription on the left leg of the colossus at Elephantine, since translated by Col. Lake.

Belzoni tells us that, before he departed for the great desert, "an English merchant, who resided in Alexandria, lent me a small house in Rosetta, near the British agency, where I left *Mrs. Belzoni.*"

Thus it may be said that the French expedition to Egypt, 1798, together with the Belzoni and Bankes explorations, 1818, were the dawn of modern Egyptology.

The French discovered the famous "*Rosetta stone*," that formed the foundation for Egyptology.

XXI. Two small obelisks of *dark-green basalt* grace the Egyptian department of the British Museum. They are known as the *obelisks of Cairo*, where the German archeologist, Niebuhr, saw and admired them. Nectanebo, who reigned from 377 to 359 B.C., raised them before the Temple of Thoth,* who was to the Egyptians what Mercury was to the Greeks and Romans. The delicately-engraved hieroglyphs on these obelisks attract much attention.

Height (only the shaft)........... 8 ft. 2 in.
Base lines of shaft............... 1 ft. 6 in. and 1 ft. 5 in.

Hieroglyphic inscriptions.

In Larousse's "*Dictionnaire Universel du XIX. Siècle*," just issued, we read: "All the obelisks known are of rose-colored granite, called syenite, which came from some quarry at Syene, in Upper Egypt." This statement is incorrect, for the two above-named obelisks are of dark-green basalt, and not of rose-colored granite. We read again in the same work: "The obelisk is peculiar to Egypt; ancient Assyrian and Babylonian civilizations seem not to have known it." Here is another mistake, for in the British Museum are two obelisks; one of them was discovered in the palace of Nimrod.

Height...................................... 5 ft. 9 in.

---

* Perhaps the Celtic god *Teutates* was derived from Thoth. Assyria had a king called *Teutanes*, and another *Teutaeus*. These Egyptian, Assyrian, and Celtic names have much analogy with the Teutones; may there not have been early connection or intercourse between the progenitors of these different races and nations? The province in Asia Minor called *Teuthrania* and *Teuta*, queen of Illyria, point in the same direction.

It is of *black marble*, covered with cuneiform inscriptions, recording the annals of the reign of Shalmanaser II. (858–823 B.C.). Instead of tapering to a point, it has three steps on the top, which seem to correspond with the three steps on the pedestal of the American obelisk, recently discovered by Commander Gorringe.

The other of the two Assyrian obelisks is of *white marble*.

Height...................................... 8 ft. 2 in.

It is covered with bas-reliefs, representing battle-scenes. It has cuneiform inscriptions, mentioning Shamas-Pul. Here are two obelisks or pillars—one is white, the other black—found in Assyrian ruins. Solomon's Temple had two pillars —*Jachin* and *Boaz*, the former white, the latter black. If Solomon's pillars have a symbolic or Masonic meaning, the Assyrian pillars may have a similar meaning. Queri: Did Assyria copy from Solomon, or did Solomon copy from Assyria? As Assyrian art antedates all others, Abraham's progeny must have copied from that of Asshur. Thus would Masonic symbols point to Assyria for prototypes. Do not the white obelisk in Nimrod's palace, 2800 B.C., Solomon's white pillar, 986 B.C., and the white stone deposited by Architect Pontius at the base of the Thothmes obelisk at Alexandria, 23 B.C., and discovered by Commander Gorringe, A.D. 1880, symbolize purity, friendship, hospitality, and thus cover a period of 4,700 years, now linking the Euphrates, Nile, Thames, and Hudson? We have lately noticed, in Assyrian illustrations, attitudes of kings that look very Masonic. Thenceforth, these hints should be thoroughly scrutinized by the Masonic fraternity.

XXII. *The obelisk of Luxor*, on Place de la Concorde at Paris. This *monolith* was transferred to France under the direction of the engineer Lebas. It stood near the little village of Luxor, residence of the kings of Thebes. Its twin stands yet in the same place, before the palace of the Pharaohs.

A vessel, named Luxor, expressly constructed at Toulon and towed to Alexandria by a man-of-war, sailed up the Nile and landed before Luxor, August 15, 1831. The taking down of the obelisk by means of apparatus, invented by M. Lebas, was successfully effected, and two months after the monolith was placed on the ship, which traversed the Mediterranean, passed the Straits of Gibraltar, coasted along France as far as Havre; then, sailing up the Seine, landed its precious cargo at Paris, in the month of September. Some months after it was erected in the centre of the Place de la Concorde, on a pedestal of granite brought from Brittany. We are told its removal and erection cost £80,000.

Whole height............................ 92 ft.
Without base, etc. (only its shaft).......... 76 ft. 4 in.
Base lines of shaft...................... 8 ft. × 8 ft.
Top lines............................... 5 ft.
Weight................................ about 246 tons.

Hieroglyphics on the four sides are admirably engraved, especially those of the three middle columns on three of the sides. The hieroglyphs on the faces north, south, and east concern Rameses II., and those on the face west Rameses III.

The veteran Egyptologist, Gustavus Seyffarth, has in his *"Summary of Recent Discoveries,"* p. 214: "*B. C.* 1831, *August* 14: *Planetary configuration at the birth of Amos II. on the Paris Monolith,"* which means, that the birthday of Pharaoh Amos II. (Rameses II. ?) corresponds to August 14, 1831 B.C.

XXIII. As the inscriptions on the pedestal of the obelisk standing on the Victoria Embankment at London give its epitomic history, we quote the whole, then add its hieroglyphs, with Dr. Sam. Birch's translation.

Transported to England and erected on this spot in the forty-second year of

QUEEN VICTORIA.

By
ERASMUS WILSON, F.R.S.
1878.
and
JOHN DIXON, C.E.

The work was further aided by
H. H. ISMAEL PACHA, *Viceroy of Egypt.*

Gen. Sir J. E. ALEXANDER.
Hon. C. H. VIVIAN.
GIOVANNI DEMETRIO.
CHARLES SWINBURNE.

JOHN FOWLER, C.E.
BENJAMIN BAKER, C.E.
H. F. STEPHENSON, C.E.
WAYNMAN DIXON, C.E.

S. BIRCH, LL.D.
GEORGE DOUBLE, *Manager of Works.*

THIS OBELISK,

HAVING FALLEN PROSTRATE IN THE SAND AT ALEXANDRIA,
WAS, IN GRATEFUL REMEMBRANCE OF
NELSON AND ABERCROMBY,
Presented to the British Nation, A.D. 1819, by
MOHAMMED ALI, *Viceroy of Egypt.*

Encased in an iron cylinder it was rolled into the Sea
August 29, 1877.

Abandoned in a storm in the Bay of Biscay,
it was recovered and taken into Ferrol Harbour, whence,
In charge of CAPTAIN CARTER, it reached
The Thames, January 20, 1878.

WILLIAM ASKEN,
JAMES GARDNER,
JOSEPH BENBOW,

MICHAEL BURNS,
WILLIAM DONALD,
WILLIAM PATAN,

Perished in a brave attempt to succour the Crew of the
Obelisk Ship, "CLEOPATRA" during the storm,
October 14, 1877.

Whole height..
Without base, etc., only the shaft......................... 68 ft. 5 in.
Base lines of shaft........................... 7 ft. 8 in. × 7 ft. 10 in.
Top lines of shaft............................ 4 ft. 10 in. × 5 ft. 1 in.
Mass or volume............................... about 2,678 cubic feet.
Weight........................... 186 tons, 7 cwt., 2 stones, 11 lbs.
Hieroglyphic inscriptions.

TRANSLATION OF THE HIEROGLYPHS ON THE ENGLISH
OBELISK.

BY SAMUEL BIRCH, ESQ., LL.D., D.C.L., F.S.A.,

Keeper of Oriental Antiquities in the British Museum.

"*First side.* Central line toward east when erected on Embankment.—The Horus, lord of the upper and lower country, the powerful bull, crowned in Uas or Thebes, the King of the North and South, Ramen Cheper, has made his monument to his father. Haremachu (Horus in the horizons), he has set up to him two great obelisks, capped with gold, at the first time of the festivals of thirty years, according to his wish he did it, the son of the Sun Thothmes (III.), type of types did it, beloved of Haremachu (Horus in the horizons) ever living.

"*First side.* Left line.—The Horus of the upper and lower country, the powerful bull, beloved of the Sun, the King of Upper and Lower Egypt, Ra-user-ma, approved of the Sun, lord of the festivals, like Ptah-Tanen, son of the Sun, Rameses, beloved of Amen, a strong bull, like the son of Nu (Osiris), whom none can withstand, the lord of the two countries, Ra-user-ma, approved of the Sun, son of the Sun, Ramessu (II.), beloved of Amen, giver of life, like the Sun.

"*First side.* Right line.—The Horus of the upper and lower country, the powerful bull, son of Tum, King of the South and North, lord of diadems, guardian of Egypt, chastiser of foreign countries, son of the Sun Ramessu (II.), beloved of Amen, dragging the South to the Mediterranean Sea, the North to the poles of Heaven, lord of the two countries, Ra-user-ma, approved of the Sun, son of the Sun Rameses (II.), giver of life, like the Sun.

"*Second side.* Central line, toward river (south), as erected on Embankment.—The Horus of the upper and lower country. The powerful bull, crowned by Truth. The King of the North and South, Ramen Cheper. The lord of the gods has multiplied to him festivals on the great Persea

The Hieroglyphs on the four sides of the London Obelisk.
(*From Champollion.*)

tree in the midst of the place of the Phœnix (Heliopolis). He is recognized as his son, a divine chief, his limbs come forth daily as he wishes, the son of the Sun, Thothmes (III.), ruler of An (Heliopolis), beloved of Haremachu (Horus in the horizons).

"*Second side.* Left line.—The Horus of the upper and lower country, the powerful bull, beloved of Truth, King of the North and South, Ra-user-ma, approved of the Sun, born of the gods, holding the two lands (of Egypt) as the son of the Sun, Ramessu (II.), beloved of Amen, making his frontier wherever he wished, who is at rest through his power, the lord of the two countries, Ra-user-ma, approved of the Sun, son of the Sun, Ramessu beloved of Amen, the lustre of the Sun.

"*Second side.* Right line.—The Horus of the upper and lower country, the powerful bull, son of the god Chepera, the King of the North and South, Ra-user-ma, approved of the Sun. The golden trait, rich in years, the most powerful; the eyes of mankind behold what he has done; nothing has been said in opposition to the lord of the two countries. Ra-user-ma, approved of the Sun, the son of the Sun, Ramessu (II.), beloved of Amen, giver of life, like the Sun.

"*Third side.* Central line, west side, as erected on Embankment.—The Horus, lord of the upper and lower country, the powerful bull, beloved of Truth, the King of the South and North, Ramen Cheper. His father, Tum, has set up to him his great name, placing it in the temple belonging to An (Heliopolis), giving him the throne of Seb, the dignity of Cheper, the son of the Sun, Thothmes (III.), good and true, beloved of the spirits of An (Heliopolis), ever living.

"*Third side.* Right line.—The Horus of the upper and lower country, the powerful bull, well-beloved of Ra, the King of the South and North, Ra-user-ma, approved of the Sun, lord of festivals of thirty years, like his father, Ptah, son of the Sun, Ramessu (II.), beloved of men, son of Tum, beloved of his loins. Athor, the goddess, directing the two countries, has given him birth, the lord of the two countries,

Ra-user-ma, approved of the Sun, the son of the Sun, Ramessu (IL), beloved of men, giver of life, like the Sun.

"*Third side.* Left line.—The Horus lord of the two countries, the powerful bull, son of Shu, the King of the South and North, Ra-user-ma, approved of Ra, the lord of diadems, director of Egypt, chastiser of foreign lands, son of the Sun, Ramessu (IL), beloved of Amen, bringing his offering daily in the house of his father Tum; nought has been done, as he did in the house of his father, the lord of the two countries, Ra-user-ma, approved of the Sun, the son of the Sun, Ramessu (II.), beloved of Amen, giver of life, like the Sun.

"*Fourth side,* and central line toward road (north), as erected on Embankment.—The Horus of the upper and lower country, beloved of the god of the upper crown, the King of the South and North, Ramen Cheper, making offerings, beloved of the gods, supplying the altar of the spirits of An (Heliopolis), welcoming their persons at the two times of the year, that he might repose through them with a sound life of hundreds of thousands of years with very numerous festivals of thirty years, the son of the Sun, Thothmes (III.), the divine ruler, beloved of Haremachu (Horus in the horizons) ever living.

"*Fourth side.* Right line.—The Horus lord of the upper and lower country, the powerful bull, beloved of Ra, the King of the South and North, Ra-user-ma, approved of the Sun, the Sun born of the gods, holding the countries, the son of the Sun, Ramessu (IL), beloved of Amen, the strong hand, powerful victor, bull of rulers, King of kings, lord of the two countries, Ra-user-ma, approved of the Sun, son of the Sun, Ramessu (II.), beloved of Amen, beloved of Tum, lord of An (Heliopolis), giver of life.

"*Fourth side.* Left line.—The Horus, the powerful bull, son of Ptah-Tanen, lord of the upper and lower country, the King of the South and North, Ra-user-ma, approved of the Sun, the hawk of gold, rich in years, the greatest of victors, the son of the Sun, Ramessu (IL), beloved of Amen,

THE OBELISK AND FREEMASONRY. 149

leading captive the Rutennu (Syrians) and Peti (Libyans) out of their countries to the seat of the house of his father, lord of the two countries, Ra-user-ma, approved of the Sun, son of the Sun, Ramessu (II), beloved of Amen, beloved of Shu, the great god, like the Sun."

"The scenes on the pyramidion represent the monarch Thothmes III. under the form of a sphinx, with hands offering to the gods Ra and Atum, the two principal deities of Heliopolis. The offerings are water, wine, milk, and incense. The inscriptions are the names and titles of the deities, the titles of Thothmes III., and the announcement of each of his special gifts."

XXIV. The *Berlin obelisk* is the earliest known. The Prussian expedition, under Lepsius, 1842, discovered it in a Memphis tomb of Manetho's 5th dynasty, which, according to Brugsch,* reigned from about 3700 to 3300 B.C. It is of limestone, and bears the name of its occupant. It seems to have been erected merely as a funeral monument, which proves that obelisks were originally used for funeral purposes.

Height, only.................................... 2 ft.

It is now in the Royal Museum, at Berlin.

Larousse tells us, in his "*Dictionnaire du XIX. Siècle,*" Augustus, and some other emperors, caused many obelisks to be transferred to Rome and Italy. We count, in our day, eleven standing in the Eternal City, and we may see the *débris* of several others which have been overthrown. Velletri, Benevento, Florence, and Cortona had obelisks standing in their squares during the Roman sway.

We here add the five obelisks now standing in Egypt.

XXV. The most ancient obelisk, erected by Pharaoh *Usurtasen* at Heliopolis, as Brugsch † tells us, "rises in the

---

* Brugsch's "History of Egypt," vol. I., p. 68.
† "History of Egypt," vol. I., p. 127.

midst of green corn-fields, in the immediate neighborhood of the village of Materieh,* consisting of a few huts of poor Arabs, and some houses of well-to-do Egyptians, who scarcely know on what famous soil their feet tread." According to Brugsch, Usurtasen I. was of the 12th dynasty of Thebes, and raised this monument to Ra about 2433 B.C. It is of the purest rose-colored syenite, and the best preserved of all the Egyptian obelisks, which is probably owing to its standing inland, away from the salt air.

Height .... 66 ft. 6 in.
Base lines of shaft............... 6 ft. 1 in. by 6 ft. 3 in.

Brugsch † speaks of its hieroglyphs as "characters deeply and beautifully cut in the red granite," and observes: ‡ "Its four sides contain hieroglyphic inscriptions of the following meaning, repeated four times in the same words:

> The Hor of the Sun.
> The life for those, who are born.
> The king of the upper and lower land.
> Cheper-ka-ra,
> the lord of the double crown,
> the life for those, who are born,
> the son of the Sun-god Ra,
> *Usurtasen,*
> the friend of the spirits of On,
> ever living
> the golden Hor
> the life for those, who are born
> the good God
> Cheper-ka-ra
> has executed this work
> in the beginning of the thirty years circle
> he the dispenser of life for evermore.

---

* Said to be the place where Joseph and Mary carried the child Jesus to escape from Herod. Hence Jesus saw this obelisk during his childhood.
    † P. 31, vol. I.   ‡ Ibid.

This four-sided inscription is terser and more expressive than any of the numerous translations we have read; so that the Egyptian Pharaohs must have grown much more prolix since their illustrious predecessor Usurtasen, whom some call Sesostris I. According to Brugsch's chronology, the Usurtasen obelisk has been standing in the same spot from 2433 B.C. to A.D. 1880, or 4,313 years, and is yet in good preservation. Where is there another instance of the kind?

XXVI. There is an obelisk at Crocodilopolis that is ascribed to Pharaoh Usurtasen I. Some attribute it to Thothmes I.

Height.................................... 43 ft.
Base lines of shaft.................... 6 ft. 9 in. by 4 ft.

Hieroglyphs.

XXVII. the highest monolith known is the obelisk at Karnak, ascribed to Hatasu, sister of Pharaoh Thothmes III., who, according to Brugsch, reigned 1600 B.C.

Whole height............................. 122 ft.
Without pedestal, only the shaft (according to
    Mariette)........................... 108 ft. 10 in.
Weight, according to Gliddon............... 400 tons.

Hieroglyphs.

XXVIII. Another obelisk at Karnak, attributed to Thothmes I.

Height...................................... 90 ft.
Base lines of shaft .... 8 ft. 1 in.
Weight, according to Wilkinson............. 297 tons.

Hieroglyphs.

XXIX. At Luxor, village near the ruins of ancient Thebes, stands the twin obelisk of the one that was carried

152   THE OBELISK AND FREEMASONRY.

to Paris A.D. 1831, and adorns now the Place de la Concorde.

Height...................................... 82 ft.

Hieroglyphs.

Explorers say there are many obelisks in Nubia, but they somewhat differ in shape from those of Egypt. They have no hieroglyphs and are of later date. Belzoni was allured to Timbuctoo by exaggerated accounts of natives, who told him of remarkable ruins and remains; consequently, he tried to penetrate that country by the Niger and lost his life.

No doubt, Egypt was the land of obelisks, many of which have been overthrown and now lie buried; for the Saracen historian, Abdallatif, tells us that he himself saw about four hundred columns of the same material lying on the margin of the sea. He relates how they came there, and that the governor of Alexandria, appointed by Saladin, had thrown down and broken those columns to construct a breakwater. "I have seen," he says, "all round the Pillar of the Colonnades remains of those columns, some entire, some broken. It was evident that those columns had been covered by a roof and cupola, which they supported." M. de Sacy translated Abdallatif's work, and called it "*Relation de l'Egypte*," see B. I., c. 4.

If this is correct, Mahometan vandalism was practised on Egyptian monuments as on the Alexandrian Library. The "Pillar of the Colonnades" here mentioned was, no doubt, the obelisk now on its way to New York. Abdallatif visited Alexandria and resided there for some time in the twelfth century of our era.

Thus did Europe value and import Oriental obelisks, which point from the Earth to the Sun and Moon, as rays dart from the Sun and Moon to Earth. The Egyptians raised them as funeral, votive, and historic monuments. For ages kings, emperors, and governments gloried in them. Lately private citizens of the Old and New World have evinced a decided taste for this graceful Egyptian structure of red granite or *syenite*, composed of *quartz*, *felspar*, and *hornblende*. Such has especially been the case among the English-speaking populations. Bankes, Wilson, Dixon, etc., have achieved wonders in England; Hurlburt, Stebbins, Gorringe, Secretary Evarts, and Consul Farman are making Herculean efforts to endow America with one of Egypt's precious relics. How this ancient form of monument has gained favor among the European races and their progeny in the Western Hemisphere may be realized in visiting *Père la Chaise, Kensal Green, Greenwood, Mount Auburn*, etc., where so many funeral tributes assume the form of graceful heavenward-pointing obelisks.

As yet, only one of the twenty-five obelisks, removed from oriental countries, has revealed the arcana of the Pharaohs to an American observer. Had Pontius, *Facundus Novus, Fontana, Lebas, Dixon*, etc., been as observing as *Belzoni* and Commander *Gorringe*, much might now be known concerning the connection between ancient, medieval, and modern Masonry. However, better late than never. Let us now interrogate the relics of the museums at Bonlac, Rome, Paris, London, Munich, Berlin, New York, and soon more light will penetrate hazy proto-historic recesses. Why the pillars at the entrance of the otherwise chaste Masonic Temple of New York terminate in a sort of wicker-work is, no doubt, best known to the projectors, who ignored the simple but graceful obelisk.

We have thus shown, that about twenty-five ancient oriental obelisks were removed to Europe, and one is on its way to the great western Republic, where Nimrod, Sesostris, Zoroaster, Pythagoras, Appolonius of Tyana, Pontius, Paracelsus, Belzoni, Lebas, Dixon, Washington, Franklin, Gorringe, etc., may, at the base of Thothmes' obelisk, shake hands and connect eastern and western Masonry by assuming the *Triangular Sun and Serpent Apron*, so significantly symbolic four thousand years ago in the rock-excavated Masonic Temple of Seti I. and Rameses II.

CHAPTER XVI.

BRUGSCH has, in his "History of Egypt," a curious list of names of royal architects, who date from the Third Dynasty to Darius I., 490 B.C. According to Gliddon, the Third Dynasty reigned about 2132 B.C. These names have been translated from hieroglyphic inscriptions. They prove that architects were usually of the royal family, or connected therewith. As these names show that operative Masonry was highly esteemed in Egypt, we give this list of Grand Masters, of whom both theoretic and operative Masons of all ages and countries may feel proud:

HEKA,* architect of the Pharaoh Senoferu.
SEM-NOFER, married to a king's grand-daughter named Amon-Zefes.
KHUFA-HOTEP, husband of the king's daughter, Hontnes.
KHUFU-ANKH.
MER-AB, a king's child, son of the Pharaoh Khufu and his wife, Setat.
PIRSON, husband of Khenshut, of the blood royal.
TI, a man of low extraction, but married to the lady Nofer-hotep, from the women's house of the king.
HAPU, architect of the Pharaoh Teta, of the Sixth Dynasty.
MERI-RA-ANK, a celebrated architect under King Pepi, of the same dynasty.
PEHEN-KA.
RA-UR.
AI.
UAH-MER.

---

* Vol. I., p. 48, Brugsch's "History of Egypt."

THE OBELISK AND FREEMASONRY.   155

*Pedigree of the Architects.**

KA-NOFER, architect of S. and N. Egypt.

IMHOTEP, architect of S. and N. Egypt, chief burgomaster, a high functionary of King Z'a-sar (lived in the time of the Third Dynasty).

R'A-HOTEP, prophet of Amon-ra, king of the gods, secret seer of Heliopolis, architect of Upper and Lower Egypt, chief burgomaster.

BOK-EN KHUNSU, chief burgomaster.

UZA-KHUNSU, architect, chief burgomaster.

NOFER-MENNU, architect, chief burgomaster.

MI (or AI), architect, chief burgomaster.

SI-NER-NEMEN-HIB, architect.

PEPI, architect, chief burgomaster.

AMON-HIR-PI-MESH'A, second, third, and fourth prophet and high-priest of Amon, king of the gods, chief burgomaster.

HOR-EM-SAF, chief burgomaster.

MERMER, architect, commander.

ZA-HIB, architect, commander.

NASSHUNU, architect, commander.

ZA-HIB, architect, commander.

NASSHUNU, architect, commander.

ZA-HIB, architect, commander.

NASSHUNU, architect, commander.

ZAN-HIBU, architect of Upper and Lower Egypt, commander.

NASSHUNU, architect.

UAH-AB-R'A RAN-UËR, architect.

ANKH-PSAMTHIK, architect of Upper and Lower Egypt.

A'AHMES SI-NIT, architect of Upper and Lower Egypt (m. SIT-NOFER-TUM).

KNUM-AB-R'A, chief minister of works for the whole country; architect of Upper and Lower Egypt in the 27th and 30th years of King Darius I. (about 490 B.C.).

---

* Vol. II., p. 299, Brugsch's "History of Egypt."

Thus this venerable body of men, styled architects and commanders, extended from 2132 to 490 B.C., or a period of sixteen hundred and forty-two years. The ancient Egyptian or Coptic word for architect was *Murket*.

We cannot help connecting with this operative Masonic galaxy the imposing ceremony of laying a corner-stone by young Pharaoh Thothmes III. at Buto, in Egypt, about 1600 B.C., and of H. R. H. Albert Edward, Prince of Wales, laying the corner-stone of Truro Cathedral, May, A.D. 1880.

The account of Thothmes' laying of the corner-stone was translated from hieroglyphs,* whereas that of Prince Albert was transmitted with lightning speed along cables and telegraph wires.

"According to the express order of the king himself, this was put down in writing; communications were orally carried on as to the erecting of a memorial building, the three sides of which bend toward the canal . . . . then I (the king) wished to place a memorial to my father, Amon-Ra, in Ape, to erect (his) dwelling, which glorifies, etc. . . .

"The (official) plan of the architect made the beginning. Never have I set out such a memorial to any other. I say that in all truth, etc. . . .

"I gave the order to prepare the cord and pegs (for the laying of the foundation) in my presence. The advent of the day of the new moon was fixed for the festival of the laying of the foundation-stone of this memorial.

"In the year 34, on the last day of the month Mekhir, on the festival of the 10th day of Amon's festival on his splendid feast of Southern Ape? . . . . . then was a sacrifice offered to the god (in) his great place. After this I went in to accompany the father Amon. The god went thither on his feet to celebrate his beautiful festival. And the Holiness of this god was wonderful to behold. [Then drew near

---

* Brugsch's "History of Egypt," Vol. I., p. 384.

the form] of this god. The cord and the pegs were ready. Then his Holiness placed me before him toward this memorial. And I began. Then was the Holiness of this god full of joy at this memorial, on account of my love for him. Then [the Holiness] of this god went further, and the beautiful feast was celebrated to my lord.

"Then I came forward, yes I, to complete the business of the laying of the foundation-stone, because .... [before] him. He went out, and the work of the first stroke of the hammer for the laying of the foundation-stone was to be performed. Then the Holiness of this divine one wished himself to give the first stroke of the hammer .... [to keep out the water] of the inundations of the fields .... of the pickaxe.

"The lines of the fields were drawn .... all that he had done. Then was I full of joy when I saw the great wonder which my father had done for me .... My heart was in a joyful humor at that beautiful procession to make a beginning of this memorial. There was laid in the foundation-stone a document with all the names of the great circle of the gods of Thebes, the gods and goddesses .... and all men rejoiced. After this .... of copper was prepared for him."

Here both the stone and the inscription break off.*

LAYING THE CORNER-STONE OF TRURO CATHEDRAL— A MASONIC PAGEANT.

THE PRINCE OF WALES GRAND MASTER OF THE CEREMONIES.

[By Cable to the NEW YORK HERALD.]

LONDON, May 22, 1880.

As the trumpets sounded the first notes of the national anthem, the cannon roared in rhythm. The Prince then ad-

---

* The whole inscription is printed in Mariette's Karnak, plate 19. Some signs in the hieroglyphic text need rectification.

vanced to lay the foundation stone, and delivered the following speech to the assembled Masons:

The Prince's Masonic Speech.

BRETHREN : We are an ancient fraternity which, from the earliest days, has been identified with all that is beautiful and grand in architecture. You will therefore be proud to have aided me, as I have been proud to work with you, in commencing a building which, by the beauty of its design and the solidity of its construction, will, we trust, be an ornament to this city and province for centuries to come. But, brethren, it is something far more than this. It is a temple to be erected to the glory and worship of our Heavenly Father, the great Architect and Creator of all things. And, whatever minor differences may be among us, I feel sure that the same spirit must be in your minds this day which animated the Jews of old, when, as Ezra tells us, the builders laid the foundations of the Temple of the Lord, and they set the priests in their apparel with trumpets to praise the Lord, after the ordinance of David, King of Israel. And they sang together in praising and giving thanks unto the Lord, because He is good, for His mercy endureth forever toward Israel. And all the people shouted with a great shout when they praised the Lord, because the foundations of the House of the Lord were laid.

Then, addressing the Bishop, His Royal Highness said:

MY LORD ARCHBISHOP, BRETHREN, AND FRIENDS : Be it known to you that we be lawful Masons, true and faithful to the laws of our country. Although not ourselves operative masons, we have from time immemorial been associated with buildings to be raised for the benefit of mankind, the adornment of the world, and the glory of the Great Architect of the Universe. We have among us secrets concealed from those who are not Masons, but they are lawful and honorable, and not opposed to the laws either of God or man. They were intrusted to Masons in ancient times, and, having been faithfully transmitted to us, it is our duty to convey them inviolate to our posterity. We are assembled here to-day in the presence of you all to erect a house for the worship of the Prince of the Most High, which we pray that God may prosper as it seems good to Him.

Emblems and Formulas.

The Prince then called upon the Grand Secretary to read the inscription on the plate over the cavity stone:

THIS CORNER STONE

OF THE CATHEDRAL CHURCH OF

ST. MARY OF TRURO

IS PLACED BY

HIS ROYAL HIGHNESS THE DUKE OF CORNWALL, K.G.,

MOST WORSHIPFUL GRAND MASTER

OF THE A. F. AND A. MASONS OF ENGLAND,

20TH MAY, 1880.

The Grand Treasurer then deposited a bottle containing coins and a copy of the Order in Council creating the See of Truro. The Earl of Mount Edgecumbe then handed the Prince a silver trowel bearing the several arms of the Grand Lodge, of the county, of the Bishop, and of the city, and of the Prince. A smooth mortar stone was lowered and the Prince applied the plumb and rule, saying:

"I find this stone to be plumb, and that the craftsmen have prepared it true and trusty."

Then he proved it by the level, saying:

"I find the stone level and that the craftsmen have labored skillfully."

Then he proved it by the square, saying:

"I find the stone plumb, level, and square, and declare it duly prepared, truly laid, and that the craftsmen have worked well."

Dedication of the Stone.

The Prince then struck the stone three times with the mallet. He scattered corn from a golden cornucopia, saying:

"I scatter corn upon the stone as an emblem of plenty and abundance, God's best gifts. May they be good seeds of His words, sown here in the hearts of men, take root and bring forth fruit hundredfold to their benefit and His glory. So mote it be."

Then, pouring wine from a golden chalice, he said:

"I pour out wine upon this stone as the symbol of strength and gladness. May those who work upon the building and those who shall hereafter meet within its walls, ever perform their allotted part in the service of the Great Architect with cheerfulness and singleness of heart. So mote it be."

Then, pouring oil from a golden vase, he said:

"I sprinkle this stone with oil as the emblem of peace and harmony. May good-will and brotherly love ever prevail among those who shall worship in this house to the glory of the Most High, until time shall be no more. So mote it be."

The Egyptian and English corner-stone laying suggests comparison. Any one inclined to compare the political and social status of Egypt under Thothmes III., 1600 B.C., and of England under Victoria, A.D. 1880, might find ample scope for poetic and historic strains. We are told Egyptian rule, under Thothmes III., extended to Mesopotamia, India, Bactria, Central Africa, and the Grecian Isles; but this is conjecture. We know that the British Empire encircles the globe, and is connected by steam, telegraph and cable, which, in a moment, flashed Prince Albert's words to the confines of the earth, whereas to convey those of Thothmes it required months and years, to say nothing of other differences.

CHAPTER XVII.

"America, the asylum for such as desire to work and be free."

THE question has been asked whether there had been secret societies like Masonry in the Western hemisphere before its discovery by Columbus, 1492. Mackenzie partly answers this question in a short article on *Mexican Mysteries*, in which he tells us: "The Mexicans (Aztecs) had religions orders and secret ceremonies like other nations." They had orders for youths and old men ; the latter, devoted to the goddess *Centcotl*, were sages, whose sayings were deemed oracular ; their number was limited, and they spent their time in making historic paintings for the instruction of the people. "The North American Indians had similar societies. Among the Algonkins there were three degrees: 1. *Waubeno ;* 2. *Meda ;* and 3. *Jossakeed.*" Humboldt found among the Orinoco Indians the order of the *Botuto*, or Holy Trumpet. The *Collahuayas* of Peru also practised secret ceremonies.

According to an ancient Mexican tradition the Indians of Chiapa had a hero called *Wodan*, or *Votan*,* whom the Great Spirit (*Teotl*) ordered to go and people the country of Anahuac or Mexico. Humboldt (in his "Monuments de l'Amérique," vol. I., p. 382) says : "This Votan, or *Wodan*, seems to be of the same family as the *Wods* or *Odins* of the Goths and the nations of Celtic origin." This tradition also states that Wodan was the grandson of a personage who, to-

---

* See p. 100, *Woden* or *Odin*.

162   THE OBELISK AND FREEMASONRY.

gether with his family, was alone saved from a universal deluge.

We might speak of Plato's *Atlantis;* of the Phenician inscription found in Brazil, which, being translated by Señor Ladislao Netto, Director of the Rio Museum, says that a Phenician colony sailed from the Red Sea and landed in Brazil about 500 B.C.; of the Icelanders, who discovered Winland (Canada) about A.D. 1001, and traded with the natives over a hundred years; of the Runic inscription on Dighton Rock, Massachusetts, which, translated by Finn Magnusen, reads: "151 Northmen occupied this land (with) Thorfins" (according to the Saga of Thorfinn this occupation happened A.D. 1007); and of prince Madoc, who sailed with a Welsh colony to the Western hemisphere 1170.

Let us begin with a custom that pervaded antiquity, medieval and modern times, and extended over the old and new world before Columbus—that custom was *Discalceation,** during certain rites and ceremonies. Jews, Christians, and Mahometans observed it. The disciples of Pythagoras were enjoined to sacrifice and worship with their shoes off. The Abyssinian Christians and Druids adhered to it. It extended even to the ancient Peruvians; and Freemasons of our day practise it in some of their rites.

We consulted Lord Kingsborough's "Antiquities of Mexico," among which we found Masonic indications like the following:

All crosses have more or less symbolic significance. The third of these Mexican ones looks like a cross of high importance in Masonry, because it is but a modification of the

---

* Taking off sandals or shoes.

THE OBELISK AND FREEMASONRY.

cross, used by the widely-diffused order of Ishmael. It has been found on Assyrian, Egyptian, Hindu, Trojan, Roman, Mexican, and Peruvian ruins. It has been called *Jaina* cross, because it is so highly cherished by the Hindu caste, named Jains. It is even found on Gothic cathedrals and fortifications of Central Europe; so that the ancient dwellers of the Western Continent must have known of its esoteric meaning.

This primitive tool, used in building Babel, Thebes, Athens, Rome, ancient Mexico, etc., has acquired a linguistic, literary, and moral significance, for Shakespeare said: "I have not kept my *square.*" Dryden: "We live not on the square." Freemasons say: "Act on the square." But let us not forget, that those great authors borrowed from Masonry.

This figure of the square, copied from Lord Kingsborough's work, is a real curiosity, when we study the signs thereon, four of which are repeated several times. Above and on the sides of these four signs are small circles, with a central dot in each. As may be observed, the dotted circles increase from one to thirteen. We think the four signs indicated the four seasons of the year, and the thirteen dotted circles around them marked the Mexican months, which must have been *lunar,* because thirteen. Thus the *Mason's square* was not only an architectural measure, but a chronologic guide with the ancient Mexicans.

As operative and theoretic Masons know the exoteric and esoteric meaning and importance of the *square,* we say no more.

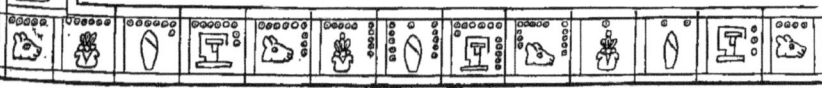

Here is Egypto-Mexican analogy in *horned disks*. In Egypt this sign was part of the royal crown, as may be seen in that of Cleopatra here. The Mexican horned disk, not being affixed to any person or object, its use and meaning cannot be inferred. This queer figure appears in several plates of Lord Kingsborough's work.

As the disk belongs to the sun and moon, it was connected with the worship of those heavenly bodies. Did Egypt borrow from Mexico, or did Mexico borrow from Egypt?

To show that there were among the American Indians indications of operative Masonry, we quote from a letter, written to us by William McAdams, Esq., of Otterville, Ill., April 25, 1880: "I have spent a considerable time during the last few years exploring our ancient mounds and earthworks, and have been surprised frequently to find mounds and earthworks resembling well-known symbols of Masonry. Some of them are thus: circles, squares, triangles; triangles and squares surrounded by circles; a circle between parallel lines:"

 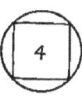

These geometric figures had primarily a practical meaning among all ancient nations; but gradually they acquired symbolic and esoteric meanings.

The triangle ever was and is now an important Masonic symbol. The equilateral triangle was adopted by most of the ancient nations as an emblem of the deity, and was regarded as the most perfect geometric figure. It occurs in Craft and Arch Masonry. In ancient and medieval magic it meant fire when the apex pointed upward, and water when the apex pointed downward. The triangle had other

THE OBELISK AND FREEMASONRY. 165

esoteric meanings, especially the one concerning the *triad*. Whether this figure had such meanings in ancient America is to be ascertained.

The same gentleman sent us "Geological History of Jersey County," Ill., in which we read, p. 112:

"Plummets.—There is another class of relics, of which great numbers are found in the mounds, and of which we have nearly a hundred in our possession. They are made of stone and iron ore. They are pear-shaped, weighing from an ounce to two or three pounds. They are with and without crease or perforation."

The cubical stone was held sacred by Hindoos, Druids, Mexicans, and Peruvians. It is also an important emblem in Masonry. The key- or central-stone of the arch in building has been found in Assyria, Egypt, Mexico, and Peru; so that operative Masonry, at least, was a craft in the Old and New World.

The three following designs are from the "Proceedings of the Davenport * Academy of Natural Sciences," vol. II., 1877. They are inscriptions on *bituminous shale*, discovered in Indian tombs by Rev. J. Gass, and described by R. J. Farquharson, M.D.:

Had a tablet like this, with designs of two *obelisks*, been found since there has been so much written and said concerning the American obelisk, it might have been considered as a joke; but as the discovery was made in 1877, when there had been no question of an Egyptian obelisk for New York, it cannot be so considered. Here two pretty well designed obelisks have their apex toward each other, and between the two apexes is an equilateral triangle, with a point in the centre.  This triangle, as previously stated, ever had an esoteric meaning in ancient religions and mythologies; so had the obelisk among the Egyptians; and

---
* Iowa.

both are Masonic emblems; hence it is not astonishing, that the symbolic triangle and obelisk found their way to a North American tribe, whose name, *Iowa*, also that of their country and river, is written and sounds like *Jehovah*. This tablet, if genuine, clearly shows that pre-Columbian dwellers

of North America had a pretty good idea of an Egyptian obelisk, and engraved it on stone, in connection with an equilateral triangle, all of which is decidedly Masonic.

This Iowa tablet could hardly be taken for anything but a zodiac, which, as Dr. Farquharson says, "suggests contact with one of the many nations or races, which have adopted that very ancient delineation of the sun's pathway through the heavens." It is evidently divided into twelve signs, which indicate twelve months and a solar year, and not thirteen months and a lunar year, as indicated on the Mexican square. The four signs like the Roman letters III, near the central circle, may indicate the four seasons, or points of the compass, or both. The central sun points to the *Philolaan* or Copernican system. The zodiac is a decided Masonic emblem. The Davenport Academy names this tablet "Calendar Stone."

This third Iowa tablet the Davenport Academy calls "Cremation Scene."

There is an Egyptian simile in Sharpe's "Texts of the Bible" (p. 208), from which we quote: "And he laid hold

THE OBELISK AND FREEMASONRY. 167

on the dragon, that old serpent, which is the Devil, and Satan, and bound him a thousand years" (Rev. xx. 2).

"This conquest of the serpent of wickedness is one of the favorite subjects in the Egyptian mythology. Our drawing is copied from the sarcophagus of Oimenepthah of

B.C. 1200; while, in note on Rev. vi. 2, we see how the same conquest was represented twelve centuries later."

This serpent procession in Egypt and among Indians in North America is a singular feature, which indicates intercourse sometime and somewhere. We cannot help thinking, that a tribe that designed two obelisks, whose pyramidions point to an equilateral triangle with a central point;—a tribe that had a zodiac and astronomic ideas connected therewith;—a tribe that had a simile to the Egyptian serpent procession; a tribe whose name *Iowa* was an analogue to the Egyptian *Y-Ha-Ho* (*the Eternal God*), to the Hebrew *Jehovah*, and to the Chinese *Yao*—must have had *arcana* they did not communicate to the world; hence that they had a certain kind of Masonry. Perhaps the *Iowa* Indians were one of the "*Lost Tribes*," who assumed the name of the *Great I am* (Jehovah), and gave it, slightly modified, to their country and river, called *Iowa* to this day, 1880. Afghanistan, Denmark, and Ireland have lately been suggested as the retreat of the "Lost Tribes."

These tablets are in the Davenport Museum, Iowa, whose trustees and members have examined them, and corresponded concerning them with the Smithsonian Institute* and American archæologists, who, in vain, sought in them alphabetic characters. Prof. Seyffarth looked for analogues to hieroglyphs, which he could not find. He thought they might be Chinese or Japanese, and therefore sent them to

---

* "Smithsonian Contributions."

savants conversant with those idioms. Schoolcraft* positively declares there never would be native alphabetic writing found on this continent, which is rather a bold assertion. We hope the recent exploring expedition to Central America, in which Mr. Lorillard figures so prominently, will disprove this declaration by discovering alphabetic characters or hieroglyphs of some kind. No doubt, the Aztec, Mexican, and Peruvian monuments and ruins will furnish some *runic, hieroglyphic, cuneiform,* or other translatable writing, that may point directly or indirectly to the origin of the primitive American races.

The pamphlet before us contains the Iowa tablets, a report thereon by Rev. J. Gass, their discoverer, and a lecture thereon by R. J. Farquharson, M.D., before the "Davenport Academy of Natural Sciences," March 9, 1877. We cite therefrom these remarks by Dr. Farquharson:

"It is objected, and seriously, too, that this discovery comes too *à propos*, too pat, in fact, and so partakes, in the minds of some, too much of the nature of a stage trick, a '*Deus ex machinâ,*' etc. . . . However, whether by fortune or misfortune, it has been our lot to make the discovery, and it now becomes our duty, honestly and firmly convinced as we are of its genuineness and authenticity, fairly to publish it to the scientific world, for its merits there to be adjudged, inviting all fair and candid criticism, yet deprecating, in the most earnest manner, the crude strictures of the hasty and inconsiderate " (vol. II., p. 103).

By these data we realize that the subject of these tablets has been considered by competent scholars, who found them worthy to be preserved among American archeologic treasures. The obelisks and equilateral triangle with a central point, the zodiac with its four cardinal points, or seasons, and the serpent procession, point directly to ancient Egypt. *Iowa,* as a derivative from Egyptian Y-Ha-Ho,

---

* "History, Conditions, and Prospects of the Indian Tribes," vol. I., p. 123.

THE OBELISK AND FREEMASONRY. 169

Hebrew *Jehovah*, or Chinese *Yao*, points to the Orient, while all but the serpent procession are Masonic signs, emblems, and symbols of high Masonic import, especially *Jehovah*.

The most interesting analogue we found during our American archeologic search for this epitome is the following:

Pharaoh Rameses II., or, Sesostris.*

Mexican Hero or Deity.†

Ardanari-Iswara, Hindu Androgyne Deity.‡

Here the serpent, or ophite symbolism, plays a conspicuous part, being a head-ornament of deity or royalty in ancient Egypt, Mexico, and India. As volumes have been written on serpent-worship and symbolism, we shall only cursorily glance at the above figures and state the comparative position of the Edenic intruder, that deceived our mother Eve. Here Rameses the Great, hero of Kadesh, sports a serpent on his forehead as a Pharaonic prerogative. The Mexican hero or god displays a serpent's head, arising from the occiput; while Ardanari-Iswara shows a serpent's head, rising from the vertex, the tail of the monster falling over the right shoulder, so that the tempter must have entered at the base of the brain, in order to emerge from the vertex. As an explanation of this singular trio would be difficult and lengthy, without being either useful or instructive, we leave this deeply esoteric subject to antiqua-

---

* See pp. 52–56.
† Lord Kingsborough's "Antiquities of Mexico."
‡ Dr. Inman's "Ancient Pagan and Modern Christian Symbolism," plate VIII. Published by James Bouton, 706 Broadway.

rians and mythologists, and content ourselves by stating, that the primitive serpent story must have expanded over an immense vista to reach from India to Egypt and distant Mexico.

This single analogy proves conclusively to our mind, that there was—somehow, sometime, and somewhere—contact, connection, and intercourse between the old and new worlds in remote ages, and that the intercourse may have been exoteric, esoteric, or even Masonic, especially when we consider that ophite symbolism is even now used in Masonry, and that it was used very extensively among the primitive races, as shown by the above serpentine trio, that extended over the world.

Archeologists have found striking analogy between the temples of Belus, in Assyria and Phenicia, and the Mexican *Teocallis*, or pyramid temples, especially that of Cholula. Humboldt speaks of this analogy in his "Monuments Américains." We have shown in this epitome, that the Egyptians and Hindus had secret or Masonic initiations in rock-excavated temples; perhaps ophite symbolism, as just exhibited, made part of those initiations and degrees, and, if so, the same ophite symbolism extended to the Mexican pyramid-temples.

What America now needs is an institution, that could take cognizance of all American archeologic, ethnologic, and philologic discoveries, in order to ascertain their genuineness and authenticity, so that authors, who write on Pre-Columbian America, might have some authority to refer to. We have in these few pages cited material enough to prove remote contact, connection, and intercourse between the Eastern and Western Continents; but there is no authority to which we can refer. Either the general government should attend to this matter, or the historic societies of the states. Perhaps some large-souled Astor, Peter Cooper, Lenox, Vassar, Girard, etc., will see the importance of such an institution, and open his heart and hand to endow it.

CHAPTER XVIII.

"The exercise of religious freedom is admitted and proclaimed to be the inalienable possession of each individual Freemason."—MACKENZIE.

FREEMASONRY, persecuted by Church and State in Europe, spread over the New World. We are aware, that Masonry was revived in the Middle Ages, and reconstructed somewhat after the system of the Dionysian architects, who, as previously stated, claimed Hiram Abif as their first grand master, about 1000 B.C. Medieval kings, popes, and bishops became leaders of Masonic guilds; but as soon as these guilds began to think for themselves, as they did at Strasburg, 1275, popes, kings, and bishops abandoned them, and soon commenced persecutions against them:

Freemasonry was interdicted in England, 1424.

Holland interdicted Freemasonry, 1735.

France tried to prevent Masonic meetings, 1737, and Gaston, Duke of Tuscany, issued an edict against the Brotherhood.

Next Pope Clement XII. fulminated a bull against the Magic Tie, 1738.

Augustus II., king of Poland, closed the lodges, 1739.

France tried again, dispersed a lodge, seized its property, and fined the landlord for renting them quarters to assemble, 1745.

Maria Theresa suppressed Freemasonry in her dominions, but her son, Joseph II., tolerated the craft. Thus had the ominous shadow been gliding for years through the imperial palaces, unknown to the Empress mother.

Even republican Switzerland proscribed the Brotherhood, 1745.

In 1748 the Sultan ordered a lodge to be demolished and its members to be arrested at Constantinople.

Pope Benedict XIV. published an edict, confirming Clement's bull, 1751.

In the same year Ferdinand VI. of Spain declared Freemasonry high treason.

A Scotch Synod excommunicated some of its members, 1757.

Francis II., Emperor of Germany, ordered lodges to be closed, 1789.

Another papal bull, issued by Pius VII., 1814, endorsed the previous hierarchic anathemas.

John VI., king of Portugal, issued a decree making Freemasonry a capital crime for natives and foreigners, 1818.

Alexander I., Emperor of Russia, published a ukase against the fraternity, 1823.

The vacillating Pius IX., himself a Mason, thought it his duty, as pope, to make an allocution to the brothers, who, in the latter part of this nineteenth century, can afford to say, with the Master: *"Father, forgive them, they know not what they do."*

While these proscriptions were issued almost over all Europe, the craft spread in the New World, and could say, with Berkeley:

> "Westward the course of Empire takes its way:
> The four first acts already past,
> A fifth shall close the Drama of the Day;
> Time's noblest offspring is the last."

We read, that the Pilgrims of Massachusetts welcomed the persecuted brotherhood in 1733; the land of Penn from 1730 to 1734; Georgia, from 1730 to 1735; New Hampshire, 1734; South Carolina, 1736; Nova Scotia, 1749; Connecticut, 1750; Rhode Island, 1750; Virginia, 1752; Jamaica Island, 1762; New York (Albany), about 1765; North Carolina, 1769; Vermont, 1781; New Jersey, 1786; Trinidad Island, 1790; Louisiana, 1793; Michigan, 1794;

Mississippi, 1801; Alabama, about 1801; Delaware, 1806; Florida, 1806; Indiana, 1807, from Kentucky; hence, Kentucky had Freemasonry prior to 1807; Missouri, 1807; Peru, 1807; Ohio, 1808; Tennessee, 1813; Maryland, 1820; Maine, 1821; Brazil, 1821; Mexico, 1825; Venezuela, 1825; Arkansas, 1832; Texas, 1836; Chili, 1841; Wisconsin, 1843; Buenos Ayres, 1846; Minnesota, 1849; California, 1850; Oregon, 1850; Canada, 1855; Washington Territory, 1858; Colorado, 1860; Nevada, 1865; Alaska, 1868; British Columbia, 1871.

Thus did Freemasonry expand from Massachusetts to Chili and Alaska in one hundred and forty-seven years; whereas it required a millennium to spread over Europe; but when we consider that Washington, Franklin, Joseph Warren, De Witt Clinton, etc., were among its first initiates in America, we cease to wonder at its rapid progress. Now Oceanica opens a promising field for Masonic expanse; already a deep interest is felt on the subject, and lodges are at work in Australia and New Zealand. India has native and foreign lodges. There is a lodge at Hong Kong, near Canton, China; also Yokohama, in Japan, has a florishing lodge.

Freemasonry has been, is, and must ever be progressive, in spite of papal bulls, royal edicts, and narrow sectarian legislation, because quiet, unostentatious charity and liberal deeds have been, are, and must be characterizing its conduct, based on these lofty qualifications, penned by the Illuminatus, Adam Weishaupt:

"Whoever does not close his ear to the lamentations of the miserable, nor his heart to gentle pity; whoever is the friend and brother of the unfortunate; whoever has a heart capable of love and friendship; whoever is steadfast in adversity, unwearied in the carrying out of whatever has been once engaged in, undaunted in overcoming difficulties; whoever does not mock and despise the weak; whoever has a soul susceptible of conceiving great designs, desirous of rising superior to base motives, and of distinguishing himself by deeds of benevolence; whoever shuns idleness; whoever, when truth and virtue are in question, despising the approbation of the multitude, is sufficiently courageous to follow the dictates of his own heart—such a one is a proper candidate."

In looking back through all history we discover, that *Masonry*, or the old associated mystic societies, analogous to modern *Freemasonry*, have been the means of promoting civilization, fostering the mechanical arts, and of holding together the more advanced minds for mutual protection and charity. The good they have quietly done in the world, seems almost incalculable. They were approved by the best men in all ages in the past. Is it not possible that, if taken up in the right spirit by the right men of the present day, it might yet be made (in the future) to yield as choice fruits as it has done in the past?

To-day, July 20, 1880, the Thothmes obelisk safely arrived in the New World, where it finds some of its country's relics, among which are the Egyptian curiosities of the New York Historical Society, and the mummy hand of Pharaoh, Seti's queen, presented to Dr. J. A. Weisse by Madame Belzoni, 1850, as mentioned pp. 63 and 64. This monolith has been the means of rectifying some historic errors and of furnishing the link that connects ancient and modern Masonry.

INDEX.

A

Abdellatif, 152.
Abel, 37, 38, 67.
Abelites, 67.
Abraham, 69, 116.
Absalom, bishop, 107.
Abydos, tablet, 137.
Adam, 37, 38.
Adoniram, 89.
Adrian, 122, 134.
Alabama, Masonry in, 173.
Alaska, Masonry in, 173.
Albert Edward, H. R. H., 106, 107, 108, 156-160.
Albertus Magnus, 110.
Alexander VII., pope, 131.
Alexander, Sir J. E., 145.
Alfred the Great, 103.
Algonkins, 161.
America, Masonry in, 172-173.
Ammian, Marc, 125, 126.
Anthemius, 100.
Antinori, 131, 132.
Antinous, 134.
Apron, Masonic, 36, 37, 39, 48, 60, 89, 153.
Apuleius, 98.
Arab Masonry, 115-121.
Architects, list of Egyptian, 154-156.
Ardanari-Iswara, 169.
Arkansas, Masonry in, 173.
Asshur, 44, 68.
Astor, 104, 170.
Athenæum, London, 4, 28.
Atlantis, 162.
Augustus, emperor, 27, 29, 97, 123, 133, 149.
Australia, 173.
Austria, Masonry in, 171.
Autopsy, 83.
Avicenna, 110.
Aztec, 161.

B

Babel, 3, 40.
Bankes, Henry, 139-141, 152.
Belzoni, 3, 8, 36-46, 60, 139-141, 153.
Belzoni, Sarah, 46, 48, 64, 65, 141.
Benedict XIV., 172.
Beneventum, 136, 149.
Berlin, 149, 153.
Berkeley, 172.
Bernard, St., 107.
Bernini, 131.
Birch, S., 4, 8, 28-34, 124, 146-149.
Blavatski, Madame, 98.
Boaz, 7, 88, 114, 143.
Boniface IV., pope, 101.
Bossuet, 106, 107.
Bouchard, 128.

Boulac, 20, 153.
Brazil, 162, 173.
British Columbia, Masonry in, 173.
British Museum, 65, 128, 141, 142.
Bruce, Robert, 107.
Brugsch, Bey, 4, 8, 72, 74, 149, 154, 156.
Buenos Ayres, Masonry in, 173.
Bunsen, 4, 8, 9, 72, 74.

C

Cain, 37, 38, 39.
California, Masonry in, 173.
Canaan, 60, 68, 69.
Canada, 162, 173.
Cartouche, 37, 48.
Centcotl, goddess, 161.
Chabas, 4, 8, 72, 73.
Champollion, 4, 8, 74, 125, 126, 128, 141.
Chiapa, 161.
Chili, Masonry in, 173.
China, Masonry in, 173.
Circle, 164.
Claudius, 123.
Clemens of Alexandria, 75, 88.
Clement V., pope, 102, 108.
Clement XI., pope, 131.
Clement XII., 171.
Cleopatra, 29, 164.
Clinton, De Witt, 111, 173.
Coffin, 71, 86, 91.
Collahuayas, 161.
Colorado, Masonry in, 173.
Columbus, 161, 162.
Compass, 3.
Connecticut, Masonry in, 172.
Congress at Strasburg, 107, 108.
Constantine, 100, 123, 137.
Constantinople, 88, 137.
Constantius, 124.
Contemporary Review, 81.
Coptic, 130, 135.
Corfe Castle, 138.
Corner-stone, laying of the, 156-160.
Crispin, St., 37.
Crocodilopolis, 151.
Cross, 162, 163.
Crusades, 78, 79, 80, 101, 108, 109.
Cuneiform, 60, 130, 142, 143, 168.
Curetes, order of, 85, 93, 94.

D

Darius I., 154, 155.
Davenport Academy, Iowa, 165, 166.
Davis, E. H., 64.
Delaware, Masonry in, 173.
Dervis, order of, 90.

INDEX.

Dighton Rock, 162.
Dionysian Architects, 87, 96, 100, 171.
Dionysian Mysteries, 86.
Diploma, papal, 101.
Discalceation, 162.
Dixon, John, 145, 152, 153.
Domitian, 7, 131.
Druids, 40, 91, 93, 162.
Druzes, 61, 115.
Dryden, 163.

E

Ebers, 4, 8.
Edda, 100.
Edwards, Amelia, 4, 61.
Egypt, Masonry in, 36–67.
Egyptian Mysteries. 70, 94.
Elephanta, 77, 78, 90, 94.
Eleusinian Mysteries, 81, 94. 95.
England, Masonry in, 103–107, 171.
Enoch, 68, 113.
Erwin von Steinbach, 107.
Essenes, 96, 109.
Eumolpus, 81.
Europe, Masonry in, 171–172.
Eusebius, 75, 88, 96.
Evarts, Hon. Mr., 2, 23, 24, 153.
Exodus, 72, 73, 74.

F

Facundus Novus, 132, 134, 153.
Faneuil, Peter, 104.
Fanton, Dr., 21, 22–23, 61.
Farman, Consul, 8, 23–27, 95.
Farquharson, R. J., M.D., 165, 168.
Florida, Masonry in, 173.
Fludd, Robert. 110.
Fontana. 123, 124, 153.
France, Masonry in, 171.
Franklin, Benj., 110, 113, 153, 173.
Frederick the Great, 110.
Free, affixed to Mason, 101, 108.
Freemasonry persecuted, 171–172.
Freemasonry spread, 172–173.

G

Gass, Rev. J., 165, 168.
Germany, Masonry in, 172.
Girard, Stephen, 104, 107.
Gladstone, 56, 57, 61.
Gliddon, George. 4, 8, 64, 73, 137, 138, 154.
Gnomon, 7, 29, 132, 133.
Goethe, 111.
Georgia, Masonry in, 172.
Gorringe, Commander, 4, 8, 13, 88, 95, 153.
Gotho-Germanic and Scandinavian Mysteries, 100.
Grand Masters (A.D. 287–1880), 103–107.
Grand Orient, order of, 61.
Gregory XVI., pope, 125.
Gustavus III. of Sweden, 111.

H

Hagar, 69, 121.
Hall of Beauties, 42, 59, 61.
Hatasu, queen, 151.
Heliopolis, 28, 149.
Herald, New York, 3, 9–23, 60, 157–160.

Hermapion, 125, 126–127, 128.
Herodotus, 8, 22, 83, 95, 122, 132, 133.
Hieroglyphs, 30–31, 145–146, 168.
Hindu Mysteries, 77.
Hiram Abif, architect, 89, 96, 171.
Hiram, King of Tyre, 88, 89.
Holland, Masonry in, 171.
Homer, 56, 57, 81.
Horned Disk, 164.
Hospitallers, order of, 101, 108.
Humboldt, A., 161, 170.
Hurlburt, 152.
Hyneman, 70, 115.

I

Iatric Freemasonry, 98.
Ictinus, architect, 83.
India, Masonry in, 77–80.
Indiana, Masonry in, 173.
Initiations, 36–37, 46. 47, 59, 78, 81, 82, 83, 86, 91, 92, 93, 94, 95, 98, 99.
Inman, Dr., 169.
Innocent X., pope, 131.
Inquisition, 84, 101, 106.
Iowa, 165, 166, 167. 168.
Ishmael, order of, 61, 69, 75, 163.
Isis, 71, 79, 87, 98.

J

Jabal, 67.
Jachin, 7, 88, 114, 143.
Jaina Cross, 162, 163.
Jamaica Island. Masonry in, 172.
Jamblichus, 100.
Japan, 62, 167, 173.
Japhet, 68.
Jehovah, 93, 166, 167, 169.
Jesus Christ, 96, 150.
Job, 69.
Jones, Inigo, 105.
Jones, Sir William, 70.
Joseph, 70, 113.
Josephus, 75, 96.

K

Kadesh, battle of, 52–55, 169.
Karnak, 151.
Kellermann, Marshal, 111.
Kentucky. Masonry in, 173.
Kheta, 52–55, 131.
Kingsborough, Lord, 162, 163, 164, 169.
Knights of St. John, order of, 101, 108.

L

Lalande, 111.
Larousse, 136, 142, 149,
Lassen, 77, 79.
Lebas, engineer, 143, 153.
Lenormant, 81.
Lenox, 104, 170.
Lepsius, 4, 8, 72, 74.
Lessing, 111.
Lévi, Éliphas, 113.
Lorillard, 168.
Lost Tribes, 70, 167.
Louisiana, Masonry in, 172.
Luke, St., 98.
Luxor, 6, 151.

INDEX. 177

M

Mackenzie, 4, 70, 77, 86, 171.
Macoy, 4.
Madoc, prince, 162.
Magi, order of, 80, 93.
Magnusen, Finn. 162.
Maine, Freemasonry in, 173.
Manetho, 8, 126, 149.
Manuscripts of Belzoni, 36-46.
Mariette, Pacha, 4, 8, 20-24, 58, 59, 72, 73, 74, 128.
Maryland, Freemasonry in. 173.
Masonry as claimed by Brethren, 67-121.
Mason's square, 3, 163.
Maspéro, 4, 8, 72, 121.
Massachusetts, Freemasonry in, 172.
McAdams, W., Jr., 164.
Melchizedek, 69.
Mesmer, 111.
Mexican Mysteries. 161.
Mexico, Freemasonry in, 173.
Michigan, Freemasonry in, 172.
Minnesota, Freemasonry in, 173.
Mississippi, Freemasonry in, 173.
Missouri, Freemasonry in, 173.
Mizraim (Menes), 45, 69.
Molay, Grand Master. 102, 108.
Moses, 8, 72, 73, 75. 76.
Mummy Hand. 63, 64.
Mysteries, Dionysian, 86.
" of Druids. 91.
" Egyptian. 70.
" Eleusinian, 81.
" Hindu. 77.
" Gotho-Germanic and Scandinavian, 106.
Mysteries, Mexican, 161.

N

Naharina, 137.
Nectanebo I., 138. 141.
Netto, Senor L., 162.
Nevada, Freemasonry in, 173.
New Hampshire, Freemasonry in, 172.
New Jersey, Freemasonry in, 172.
New York, Freemasonry in, 172.
New Zealand, Freemasonry in, 173.
Nibelungen, 100.
Nimrod, 68, 142, 153.
Noachites, order of, 68.
Noah. 44, 68.
North Carolina, Freemasonry in, 172.
Nova Scotia, Freemasonry in, 172.
Nubia, 152.
Numa Pompilius, 94.
Nuncoreus, 122.

O

Obelisks for New York, 1-35.
" at Rome, Piazza St. Peter, 122.
" " Santa Maria Maggiore, 123.
" " St. John Lateran, 123.
" " Porta del Popolo. 124.
" " Piazza Navona, 131.
" " Piazza della Minerva, 131.
" " del Monte Cavallo, 131.
" " Trinita del Monte, 132.
" " Monte Citorio, 132.
" " Monte Pincio. 134.
" " Villa Mattei, 135.
" " Circus Flora, 135.

Obelisks at Catana, Sicily. 135.
" at Beneventum, 136.
" at Arles, France, 136.
" at Constantinople, 137.
" " " 138.
" Egyptian, in British Museum, 141.
" Assyrian, " " 142.
" at Paris, France, 143.
" at London, on Victoria Embankment, 144.
Obelisks at Berlin, 149.
" at Heliopolis, Egypt, 149.
" at Crocodilopolis, Egypt, 151.
" at Karnak, Egypt, 151.
" at Luxor, Egypt, 151.
Oceanica, 173.
Ohio, Masonry in, 173.
Oregon, Masonry in, 173.
Ormus, 109.
Osirtasen or Usurtasen, 70, 149, 150, 151.

P

Paracelsus, 110, 153.
Parsees, 61. 69, 80.
Paul, St., 98.
Peleg, 69.
Pennsylvania, Masonry in, 172.
Pentaour, poem. 52-55.
Perpendicular, 3, 43.
Persecution of Freemasonry, 171-172.
Peru, 161. 162, 163, 165, 173.
Phidias, 84.
Philæ, 138.
Philippe le Bel, 102, 108.
Pierret. 72.
Pius VI., pope, 131.
Pius VII., 134, 172.
Pius IX., 111, 172.
Plate nineteenth, initiation, 46.
Plato, 8, 95, 162.
Pliny, 7, 8, 122, 133.
Plummet, 3, 165.
Plutarch, 81, 98.
Poland, Masonry in, 171.
Pontius. architect, 24, 26, 27, 97, 143, 153.
Poole, 4, 74.
Porta, Battista, 110.
Portugal, Masonry in, 172.
Psammitichus, 74, 133.
Psammuthis, 60.
Pythagoras, 8, 85, 94, 100, 153, 162.

Q

Quakers, 80.

R

Rameses II. (Sesostris), 3, 6, 36, 37, 48, 52-55. 60, 71, 72, 73, 77, 85, 88, 90, 94, 113, 131. 144, 146, 169.
Rameses III., 6, 144.
Rawson, Dr., 4, 115-121.
Rénan, 22. 121.
Report on New York Obelisk by S. A. Zola, 11-20.
Rhode Island, Freemasonry in, 172.
Rosellini, 72, 74. 125, 128, 141.
Rosetta Stone, 128-130, 141.
Rosicrucians, 100, 101, 109.
Rougé, De. 8, 72.
Runic, 162, 168.
Russia, Freemasonry in, 172.

INDEX.

S

Saladin, 152.
Salt, Consul, 139.
Schoolcraft, 168.
Seth, 39, 67.
Seti I. (Osymandias), 3, 36, 58, 60, 71, 72, 77, 85, 91, 94, 113, 153.
Seti II. (Menephtah), 72, 74.
Seyffarth, 4, 8, 49, 60, 72, 74, 125, 128, 167.
Shakespeare. 163.
Shalmanaser II., 142.
Sharpe. 166.
Sidon, 68.
Sixtus V., pope, 122, 123, 124.
Smithsonian Institute, 167.
Socrates, 83.
Solomon. 7, 88, 89, 114.
Sophia, St., 100.
Sotheran, C., 109.
South Carolina, Freemasonry in, 172.
Spain, Freemasonry in, 172.
Spohn, 4, 8.
Square, Mason's, 3, 163.
Squiers, George, 64.
Stebbins, Henry, 152.
Strabo, 8, 75, 76, 83, 136.
Strasburg, Congress of, 107-108.
Swedenborg, 111.
Switzerland, Freemasonry in, 171.

T

Tacitus, 8.
Templars, order of, 101, 107, 108, 109.
Temple, Masonic, 8, 36, 47, 60, 77, 85.
Tennessee, Freemasonry in, 173.
Teocallis, 170.
Teotl, Great Spirit, 161.
Teutonic Knights, order of, 101, 108.
Texas, Freemasonry in, 173.
Theodosius, 84, 137.
Thorfinn, 162.
Thothmes I., 151.
Thothmes III., 28-34, 36, 72, 124, 137, 146, 156.
Thothmes IV., 124.
Tomlinson, Rev. G., 125.
Translation of hieroglyphs, 31-34, 146-149.
Triangle, 43, 164, 165.
Trinidad Island, Freemasonry in, 172.
Truro Cathedral, 156-160.

Tubal-Cain, 67, 113.
Turkey, Freemasonry in, 172.

U

Ungarelli, 125, 126, 128.
Usher, 72, 74.

V

Vassar, 170.
Venezuela, Freemasonry in, 173.
Vermont, Freemasonry in, 172.
Victor, P., 137.
Victoria, Queen, 144, 145, 160.
Virginia, Freemasonry in, 172.
Vitruvius, 96.
Voltaire, 7, 111.

W

Warren, Joseph, 111, 173.
Washington, George, 111, 112, 153, 173.
Washington Territory, Freemasonry in, 173.
Weishaupt, A., 173.
Weisse, Jane Lee, ode to the obelisk, 34-35.
Wilkinson, 4, 72, 74, 151.
Wilson, Erasmus, F.R.S., 145, 152.
Wisconsin, Freemasonry in, 173.
Wodan, Woden, Votan, Odin, 100, 161.
World, New York, 3, 23-27.
Worth Monument, 8.
Wren, Sir Christopher, 105, 112.

Y

Yao, 167, 169.
Y-Ha-Ho, 167, 168.
Yokohama, 173.
Young, Dr., 4, 8, 42.

Z

Zendavesta, 80.
Zodiac, 166, 168.
Zoëga, 132, 133, 134.
Zola, S. A., 9-20, 61, 77, 95, 97.
Zoroaster, 80, 153.

www.ingramcontent.com/pod-product-compliance
Lightning Source LLC
Chambersburg PA
CBHW040312170426
43195CB00020B/2943